bratwurst and bicycles

by

Steven Herrick

Text copyright 2014 Steven Herrick
PO BOX 640
Katoomba, NSW, 2780.
Australia.

All Rights Reserved

Eurovelo Series Book Three

The moral right of the author has been asserted. This book is copyright. Except for private study, criticism or reviews and research, as permitted under the Copyright Act, no part of this book may be reproduced, or transmitted in any form or by any means without the prior permission of the Author and Publisher.

Cover photograph by Steven Herrick
Also published as a paperback by CreateSpace 2014.
ISBN - 13: 978-1503135260
ISBN - 10: 1503135268

Eurovelo Series Book One: *'baguettes and bicycles'* published by
Amazon and CreateSpace in 2012.
Eurovelo Series Book Two: *'bordeaux and bicycles'* published by
Amazon and CreateSpace in 2013.

Table of contents:

About the Author
Introduction
Chapter One: Basel to Bad Sackingen
Chapter Two: Bad Sackingen to Singen
Chapter Three: Singen to Meersburg
Chapter Four: Meersburg to Lindau and return
Chapter Five: Lindau to Sigmaringen
Chapter Six: Sigmaringen to Ulm
Chapter Seven: Ulm to Lauringen
Chapter Eight: Lauringen to Neuberg an der Donau
Chapter Nine: Neuberg an der Donau to Neustadt an der Donau
Chapter Ten: Neustadt an der Donau to Regensburg
Chapter Eleven: Regensburg to Deggendorf
Chapter Twelve: Deggendorf to Passau
Chapter Thirteen: Passau to Wesenufer
Chapter Fourteen: Wesenufer to Linz
Chapter Fifteen: Linz to Ardagger Markt
Chapter Sixteen: Ardagger Markt to Grein
Chapter Seventeen: Grein to Melk
Chapter Eighteen: Melk to Tulln
Chapter Nineteen: Tulln to Vienna
Chapter Twenty: Vienna to Bratislava
Chapter Twenty-one: Bratislava to Velky Meder
Chapter Twenty-two: Velky Meder to Sturovo
Chapter Twenty-three: Sturovo to Budapest

About the Author

Steven Herrick is the author of twenty-one books for children and young adults. In Australia, his books have won the New South Wales Premier's Literary Award in 2000 and 2005 and the Western Australia Premier's Literary Award in 2013. His books have also been shortlisted for the prestigious Children's Book Council of Australia Book of the Year Awards on seven occasions. He is published in the USA by Simon and Schuster and Boyds Mill Press. He has also been published in the UK and The Netherlands.

Steven has written travel articles, features and restaurant reviews for newspapers and magazines and regularly travels the world performing his poetry and conducting author talks in schools. He lives in the Blue Mountains in Australia with his wife Cathie, a belly dance teacher. They have two adult sons, Jack and Joe.

This is his third travel book, following on from the successful *'baguettes and bicycles'* and *'bordeaux and bicycles.'*

www.stevenherrick.com.au

dothebikething.blogspot.com.au

Introduction

I have been in Basel, Switzerland for the past two days. The city mixes industry and commerce with a friendly small-town vibe which is quite an achievement for a place that straddles the border of three countries. Its schizophrenic location gives rise to a welcoming and cosmopolitan outlook.

I have contentedly cycled back and forward across the numerous bridges spanning the Rhine, regularly overtaken by handsome people on hip bicycles wearing all manner of inappropriate cycling garb with a style reserved for the young and the beautiful.

Last night, in my Bed and Breakfast overlooking the Swiss-French border, I spread the map of Europe out on the kitchen table and traced a line with my finger from Basel east along the Rhine River before linking with the Danube and wiggling all the way across to Budapest in Hungary. The Euro Velo 6 bike path through Germany, Austria, Slovakia and Hungary beckoned. How could I refuse?

My bicycle, nicknamed Craig after the surname of a famous weight-loss guru, waited in the shed, no doubt thrilled at the prospect of lugging me and my panniers two thousand kilometres across Europe.

Craig and I have enjoyed previous European adventures, cycling across France from west to east, documented in my book 'baguettes and bicycles' and following the canals of Southern France which featured in 'bordeaux and bicycles.'

He's been such a trustworthy companion that I'd surprised him with the gift of a new front tyre on arriving safely in Switzerland. I'd also given him a polish with a rag to have him looking his best for our new adventure. Everyone feels better after a good scrub down, even a somewhat moody red hybrid bicycle.

Cordula, the friendly owner of the Bed and Breakfast welcomed us with a smile, numerous cups of coffee and the delicious local biscuits called Basler Lecklei baked with cinnamon, honey and spices. Craig seemed content in his shed, standing upright between two sturdy Swiss bikes and a grizzled lawn mower.

I spent my first day in Basel at the Swiss International School, talking to the students. For the past twenty-five years, I have made a living as a poet. I kid you not. Poetry has been very good to me. I have written twenty-one books for children and young adults and visited schools from Zagreb to Malaga; Stockholm to Sydney; Vancouver to Kuala Lumpur. The students in Basel, from twenty-seven different countries, were like young people everywhere - welcoming, inquisitive and optimistic. Another perk of my perfect job - I get to meet such thoughtful and engaged citizens of the world.

The following day I wandered the streets of Basel eating bulky sandwiches and cherry strudels washed down with strong coffee while watching the townsfolk go about their day. My favourite location was a bench seat in the town square, listening to the trams rumbling across the cobblestones. My childhood hometown of Brisbane in Australia had trams. I was always captivated by their breezy openness, the hard wooden seats and their curious waltz-like clatter across intersections.

In Basel, I ate too much, perhaps fortifying myself for the journey ahead? The great French leader, Napoleon Bonaparte said, 'An army marches on its stomach.'

The same can be said of the cyclist. My body needs substantial fuel to satisfy the demands of riding many kilometres each day and one of the great joys of long-distance cycling is that I can indulge in the culinary delights of the villages, cities and countries I ride through.

Or as my wife succinctly puts it, 'cycling is just an interlude between meals.'

This book is an exploration of a cycle route from Basel to Budapest - the landscape, the people, the culture and history - and its food. I planned to eat as much as possible every evening and take it out on Craig the next day. My bicycle friend really was better than any diet. I've found that eighty kilometres a day on Craig gave me freedom to indulge. And what I wanted to indulge in was European food, in all its guises from schnitzel to strudel, pork to potato cakes, goulash to gateaux.

Ahead of Craig and I were four weeks of German and Eastern European adventures. In seven days time, we also had the arrival of my wife, Cathie who planned to join us in Ulm for the long cycle down the Danube. I'd promised Craig a surprise. He was getting a bike companion. I'd be buying Cathie a sleek drop-bar European bike who we planned to name Jenny, to accompany Craig. Now he had someone to talk with!

I can hear Craig sighing from the shed, although it may be the sound of wind in the trees. Tomorrow, we begin our adventure.

Chapter One:

Basel to Bad Sackingen, Germany

After a fortifying breakfast of muesli, toast and espresso, Cordula wishes us a pleasant journey while waving from the open window as I point Craig towards the bright sun rising across Europe, pat his crossbar and say, 'East.'

Basel wakes to the warm sunshine of a perfect spring day as I languidly pedal down the Elsasserstrasse, careful not to get my tyres caught in the tram tracks. A middle-aged couple walk hand-in-hand along the footpath. They are both dressed in white slacks and matching blue open-necked shirts. The man nods good morning.

Bikes are chained and locked outside many of the four-story apartment buildings. A young man, shirtless and with a long ponytail wheels a green barrow haphazardly across the street. It's empty. I can't imagine what he plans to fill it with? Groceries? Perhaps discarded junk he'll scavenge down by the river? We exchange greetings and he expertly flips the barrow over the gutter and back onto the footpath.

I cross the Johannite Bridge and within a few minutes - drum roll, please - Craig and I enter Germany. For a citizen of an ocean-locked nation like Australia, it still gives me a thrill to pedal across the border between countries.

In Rheinfelden, there is a Saturday market with stalls offering giant loaves of hard crusted bread; a cornucopia of sausages, salami, farm eggs, fruit and vegetables and most prominent of all, tables laden with cakes and strudels. Gruff old ladies in serious frocks fill shopping trolleys with enough food to feed a German village.

I cross the Rhine to the neighbouring Swiss town, also called

Rheinfelden where there's another market although not as well-attended as its German counterpart. Most of the Swiss seem content to drink coffee in outdoor cafes rather than load up on supplies. The Swiss town is much older and prettier than its German brother. Flagpoles line the bridge, apartments display window boxes overflowing with greenery, a park fountain spurts three loops of water vigourously into the morning as Craig and I bounce over ancient cobblestones.

I continue along the Swiss side, deep into a forest above the Rhine with extended views up river to a dam. Swans swim close to the bank oblivious to the chimney stacks and chemical plants in Germany. The hills on this side are heavily forested. The Swiss have red bike markers, the Germans blue, and neither seem to worry too much about telling me I'm on Euro Velo 6. They use their own numbers and as I'm without a trail map, I'm happy just to keep sight of the Rhine.

Downwind of a fertilizer factory, I see my first stork of the season. Such a giant bird with a corresponding size nest, they are highly respected as a sign of good luck, meaning no-one disturbs their home. So the stork builds wherever it damn pleases. I like that. This stork has chosen the top of a disused old chimney. Despite the surrounding smell, I watch the bird sitting proud surveying her domain.

I have deliberately planned an easy day cycling today to ease myself back into the daily grind of touring. Consequently I spend an inordinate amount of time wandering aimlessly on Craig. We cycle through the Swiss village of Wallbach, admiring the obvious wealth and restrained civility. Every garden is immaculate, the streets are clean, expensive cars are driven at an orderly pace through town. I'm afraid to sweat should I be fined for public unruliness. Craig seems quieter than usual, his creaks and rattles muted.

On a wide sweeping bend in the Rhine, I look across to the town of Bad Sackingen, made famous in the 19th Century novel, *The Trumpeteer of Sackingen* by German author Joseph Victor von Scheffel.

Bad Sackingen is a gem of a town with the entry from the Swiss side via the longest covered bridge in Europe.

I've loved covered bridges ever since I rode across them in the Amish districts of Pennsylvania twenty-six years ago. This one is so long it has a slight kink at one end. I ride back and forth a few times before I notice there is a white borderline painted across the middle of the bridge. I dismount from the bike and put one foot either side of the line. 'Look, everybody, one foot in Germany, one in ...'

Sorry, I'm indulging.

You have to admire a covered bridge with window boxes, red flowers blooming cheery in the midday sun. I cross the bridge once more, delighting in the shade of the wooden structure, the cool breeze blowing down the Rhine, the scent of flowers. I notice that every person I pass wears a smile, as though stepping onto this structure immediately brightens our day.

I cycle along the riverbank and complete a quick lap of the town before choosing a Gasthaus in the village square to have lunch. All of the outdoor tables are taken, but I've had enough sun for today so I'm happy to relax in a large booth framed by a window peering out to the 18th century St Fridolin's Cathedral where a wedding is taking place. I eat a hearty schnitzel and potatoes, washed down with the local beer, keeping watch for the bride and groom.

Music blares from the square as the church doors swing open and the happy couple stride into newly-married sunshine. I leave my meal and walk outside to snap a photo and enjoy the celebration. Who doesn't love a wedding? We all applaud as they board a carriage and are driven off to the reception. The bride giggles, the groom waves regally.

After another beer, I walk across the square and enter the Cathedral. Wow! I have never seen such an overblown confection of a church interior. The ceiling has intricate baroque paintings featuring ... well, everything really. Lots of cherubs, some holding grapes, some offering flowers; Cupid shoots his arrow; animals peer down on the parishioners; half-clothed pilgrims reach out wanting to touch God, I imagine. The colour scheme is blindingly white, apricot and blue and it's all so three-dimensional and over the top. I wonder if there's a more perfect location for a wedding in the world?

I return later in the afternoon for a second look. This time I notice the sculptures of cherubs on the ceiling. On the side walls of the Cathedral are the Stations of the Cross, but these paintings seem mute compared to what's going on above. The image of being inside a giant wedding cake comes to mind.

I'm so early to my hotel today that I just drop my bags and go for a cycle up a Category Two mountain outside of town. I know I said I didn't want to exert myself, but I'm so invigorated by the wedding scenes and the lovely village, that sitting in a hotel room just doesn't make sense. It's a short climb of only four kilometres, but very steep. The scent of pine hangs thick in the air and the huge trees shade the narrow road, keeping me cool. On top of the hill I have views of the Rhine Valley with its forested slopes, acres of farmland and pockets of industry. I cycle around the small village. Once again, I'm struck by the apparent wealth and orderliness, even on the German side of the Rhine.

The descent is suitably bracing, gliding all the way to my hotel. Craig is given a locked garage for the night, to share with two hulking motorcycles. I pat his seat and tell him to play nicely.

In the evening, I eat in the hotel restaurant. The waitress, a big-boned young woman with curly brown hair and wearing a flouncy blue dress brings me a little bowl of 'pork in jelly,' free from the kitchen. I love that. It always sets up a meal nicely, it doesn't matter how small the gift is, it's the thought that counts.

This tasty morsel is followed by a large salad to start, smothered in a creamy dressing, tasty but overwhelming. For my main course, the waitress brings a brass-plated saucepan full of veal and mushroom stew and a plate-size portion of rosti. She cuts half the rosti and ladles generous helpings of the veal on top. My large plate is full. She then puts a lid on the saucepan and a cover over the remaining rosti, leaving both dishes on a warming tray in the centre of the room. I eagerly devour the meal. The rosti is sensational, crisp and buttery and it soaks up the cream sauce of the veal. I lean back, satisfied. One more beer is in order.

After bringing my pilsener, the waitress takes my plate and refills it with the remaining rosti and veal from the saucepan. She smilingly returns the full plate to my table. She expects me to eat a second main course? At lunch, I'd noticed the portions were large, but this is heart-attack territory.

I sigh contentedly, before embarking on my second serve. I manage to eat half the meal. I can't move for an hour afterwards. The waitress asks me if I want dessert and seems disappointed when I politely say no.

I fear my dreams tonight will be of being stuck inside a wedding cake and having to eat my way out.

Accommodation: Hotel zer Fluh, Weihermatten 40, Bad Sackingen. Located one kilometre from the city centre, near a number of health clinics in a quiet suburban backstreet. A clean, comfortable hotel in peaceful surroundings, friendly hosts, free wifi, garage for bicycles, excellent breakfast. My score: 16/20.

Restaurant: Hotel zer Fluh Restaurant. Huge portions of traditional German schnitzels, stews and rosti. Friendly owners.

What more could you want? If you're a light eater, perhaps order one course between two! My score: 15/20.

Route tips: It's easy and fun to cycle for a short time on the German side of the Rhine before switching to the Swiss. Perhaps it's a little harder finding your way on the Swiss side, but worth it as there's more forest tracks and less industry. If you're on a budget, cross back to the German side to eat and sleep as it's much cheaper. Ride across the covered bridge at Bad Sackingen, again and again.

Distance cycled today: 42 km

Actual distance: 36 km

What I should have said: 'Dear Fraulein, one plate of food will suffice, danke.'

Chapter Two:

Bad Sackingen to Singen, Germany.

If I was surprised by the size of the dinner last night, with a one hundred kilometre cycle ahead today, I'm prepared for breakfast. The same friendly waitress, now dressed in more casual attire of jeans and a white blouse, directs me to the self-serve array. And what a smorgasbord it is - muesli, juice, fruit, yoghurt, thick brown bread and a boiled egg.

I ask Craig if he slept well and he squeaks in response. I get the impression he was overawed by the large black motorcycles. I hope they didn't taunt him because of his lack of an engine.

'I'm your engine, Craig,' I say.

He bumps awkwardly over a tree route protruding through the bitumen to remind me that it takes more than just power to cycle across Europe. One needs guile and vision as well. I promise to do better.

The morning is sunny and cool as we roll unsteadily through Bad Sackingen. The Rhine is a fetching pea-green colour as it meanders through a narrow valley. I stick to the German side, barely rising above 15 kilometres per hour. Craig creaks under the increased weight of rosti, stew and an Ironman breakfast. After forty minutes, I cycle up a large hill affording a lovely view of the historic village of Laufenburg on a bend in the Rhine. It's so enticing, I turn right and speed downhill to the stone bridge. The cobblestones slow my descent somewhat. I tentatively roll through what is undoubtedly a popular tourist village, with a swank hotel near the entrance to the town. The village shops, closed at this hour, display all manner of alluring trinkets.

After much shaking and cursing, Craig and I wobble onto the bridge over the Rhine separating the German and Swiss villages, both named Laufenburg. They were one town until 1800 when Napoleon divided them, making the border the centre of the river where I'm now standing. It's a glorious scene.

On the Swiss side are houses of mute grey or green fronting the river. A couple on the third floor balcony have breakfast and watch the strange man on the bridge taking photos of himself. I can smell the coffee wafting from their kitchen. Behind the houses rises a white-painted church steeple with a red-faced clock that informs me it's only 9am. The Swiss village is surrounded by green forested hills.

On the German side the houses are painted in similar conservative colours. A walking path leads in front of the houses along the river. Rising above this village is a much more austere church, built on the hill. On the northern bend in the river is a statue of an eagle clasping a Christian Cross in its talons, ready to take flight swooping low over the villages perhaps to remind them of the power of the Church?

The bridge itself is decorated with ornate street lamps. Concrete flower boxes have been installed at either end to allow only bicycle and pedestrian traffic. Very civilised. There are trees offering shade along the length of the twin bridge spans. A woman, wearing clothes in similar plain colours to the houses, walks past me nodding good morning. I notice she's wearing bright white ankle socks and trainers even though she appears to be on a gentle morning stroll. Perhaps to exercise in such bucolic surroundings would be too insulting. I can only agree, so I reluctantly push Craig back into Germany and up the cobblestone main street.

Once atop the hill, I plot a crooked route attempting to stay as close to the Rhine as possible. A few kilometres from Laufenburg, I cycle through a small village with a white painted church topped with a brown wooden steeple. It's perfectly proportioned and sits beside an equally inviting fir tree. Further along the road is an old wooden barn, sharing the same symmetrical fluidity as the church. What a lovely place to live, with the Rhine flowing swiftly one hundred metres away. Back on the river path, I notice a number of long boats ahead of me. Each boat has five occupants and one man standing and steering. It looks like a group expedition for tourists. A few even deign to take my photo. I sit more upright than usual and wave.

After thirty kilometres of cycling along the German side, I somehow find myself lost in Switzerland, without even having crossed the river. It's all very confusing. Lunchtime is upon me and I don't really want to eat in Switzerland with the hassle of paying in Euros and getting Swiss Francs as change. To tempt me even more a weinfest is being held at Rafz. Scores of people are sitting at long bench tables at the entrance to a large barn. The smell of barbecue smoke drifts across my path. Only a moment ago, I saw my first Rhine vineyard in Switzerland. And yet I've never heard of Swiss wine. Rafz is a lovely town of houses with wide wooden crossbeams and sturdy roofs. Many dwellings have window-boxes full of flowers and old-fashioned shutters on each window. One bright yellow house has a sundial attached to its southern wall. It's an hour slow. Perhaps allowing for daylight saving?

My stupid mobile keeps alerting me through text messages that I've entered Switzerland. Or Germany. Or Switzerland. It's as confused as I am.

Then all of a sudden I'm back in Germany. In a small village beside a train track, I cycle the streets looking for somewhere to eat. There is only one Gasthaus, with three outdoor tables. One table is occupied by two leather-clad bikers drinking beer. I quickly look at their motorbikes. Yep, big and black. I make sure I park Craig as far away from them as possible.

At the second table, a family of four are eating schnitzels and chips. I take a seat at the vacant table and am quickly greeted by the large gruff owner who explains there is only schnitzel and chips. I order a serve and a beer. It's pleasant to sit in the sun listening to the conversation of groups of people, none of which I can understand. The family appear to be discussing an issue with the teenage son, with lots of gestures and finger-pointing. The boy tries to focus on eating his chips, while his Mother offers a long lecture. The father drinks his beer and nods agreement. The daughter smiles smugly, perhaps pleased she's not the centre of attention. My schnitzel arrives and predictably, it's huge with chips cascading off the plate onto the plastic table. I wolf it down, aware that I still have forty kilometres to cycle this afternoon.

At Schaffhausen, a Swiss town on the Rhine, I get lost while admiring the fine Renaissance buildings. I end up in a near-deserted bus station. I ask the young woman reading a glossy magazine if she knows the way to Singen. She bites her bottom lip before pointing down the hill. She looks decidedly uncertain but it would be rude to deliberately pedal in the opposite direction, so I thank her and set off. Sure enough, I'm lost again within ten minutes. I cycle along suburban roads, eagerly looking for street signs. Finally an arrow points to the right for Singen and I gratefully join a bicycle path beside a busy road.

I'm quickly learning that the infrastructure of Germany regularly offers independent bicycle paths beside roads. In France, the paths are either beside a river or canal or are part of the main road, only separated by a white line. In my home of Australia, cyclists have to battle with vehicles on haphazardly marked roads, where the white line separating cars and bikes disappears without warning or doesn't exist at all. We have an alarmingly high rate of cyclist deaths because of these third-world conditions. It is a pleasure here in Germany to be cruising along on my own path, the speeding vehicles and I separated by a few metres of garden.

I cycle into Singen in the late afternoon. My hotel is in the centre of town. The streets are very quiet with just a few people enjoying an afternoon stroll. Some of the streets are pedestrian-only and the city centre is full of closed shops and signs advertising upcoming sales. On the way in, I noticed a few Gasthauses with people sitting outside drinking beer, but few other places to eat. I'd like to avoid schnitzel tonight. Luckily, the young man at hotel reception speaks fluent English and recommends a Turkish restaurant a few blocks away.

I stroll the evening streets, bone weary and hungry. The Bosphorus Restaurant has a take-away section serving coffee and pizzas and a yellow-walled restaurant with big comfy chairs offering more traditional Turkish fare. I opt for a table under a large mirror and eat my fill of chicken kebab, rice and salad. It's fresh, spicy and filling, just what I needed. I raise a glass in honour of all the Turkish immigrants in Germany, particularly the mercurial Mesut Ozil. Food and football. Sehr gut!

Accommodation: Hotel Victoria, Hegaustrasse 40, Singen. Pleasant hotel with a basement room for bicycles, English-speaking staff. Try to avoid booking a top-floor room as noise from the kitchen exhaust fans can intrude. Good breakfast, but you must pay for wifi. My score: 13/20.

Restaurant: Bosphorus Restaurant, Erzbergerstrasse 13, Singen. A good quality budget alternative to heavy German food. The portions are large, service is brisk and atmosphere is easy-going. My score: 14/20.

Route tips: Certainly take the time to visit Laufenburg. Perhaps even consider staying a night there. The path along the Rhine is mostly hard-packed gravel, so wide tyres are useful. The beauty of this region is to be found in the tiny villages, either side of the border.

Distance cycled today: 96 km

Actual distance: 84km

What I should have said: 'May I join you for coffee on the balcony, bitte?'

Chapter Three:

Singen to Meersburg, Germany

After a fitful night spent sleeping under the whirring sound of a kitchen exhaust fan, I stumble down to breakfast and eat large portions of muesli and solid rye bread. Yes, I will have a second boiled egg, danke.

Today is a public holiday and everyone has decided to ride with me to Lake Constance. It's like Parramatta Road - sorry, obscure Australian traffic reference - for bicycles. Middle-aged couples on sit-up bikes wobble along the track, children pedal furiously past them, an old man on a ramshackle three-speed tourer whistles as he rides, and I weave Craig awkwardly between them all.

After Radolfzell, the path winds alongside the lake and a train track. Vineyards patchwork the gentle slopes rising from the shoreline. I regularly stop to gaze across the water to the Swiss side of the lake. Wooden piers jut into the still water, a lone boat putters in the shallows and the peloton of senior citizens winds its way to Konstanz. I accept my lanterne rouge duties at the rear of the pack and slowly we pedal into town.

Whoa! So this is how Germans spend their public holiday! Every restaurant has outdoor tables packed with beer-drinking, pink-faced holidaymakers. The smell of fried food and suntan lotion hangs in the air. I cycle to the water's edge. Konstanz bulges under the pressure of so many people. The constant click of camera shutters accompanies my lunch of bratwurst on a roll and a beer, bought from a cycle van set up for the day on the promenade.

I sit on the grass under a tree and watch a mother try to get her toddler son to stand still for a photo with the majestic lake as a backdrop. He just wants to run into the water. Can't say I blame him. It's a scorching hot day, with too much white flesh on display among the sun worshippers on the stone wall of the promenade.

Boats of every shape and style jostle near the marina. Tourist paddleboats the size of speedboats move surprisingly briskly in the shallows. For someone from the hottest continent on earth, it's unusual to see so few people wearing sunhats. I relax in the shade and watch the statue of Imperia slowly revolve on her pedestal at the entrance to the harbour. In one hand, the nine-metre high Courtesan holds the King, in the other the Pope. Both men are naked except for the crown and Papal tiara. Created by Peter Lenk and erected in 1993, Imperia slyly commemorates the Council of Constance that took place here in the early 15th Century. Based on a satire by Honore de Balzac, Imperia is a humourous and irreverent presence on the lake.

Konstanz is a lovely town of 80,000 residents that retains many of its historic buildings due to its fortuitous location on the Swiss border, which meant it escaped the aerial bombings of World War Two.

As if on cue, Imperia is buzzed overhead by an advertising zeppelin for the Bregenzer Festspiele, a annual arts festival held in the Austrian lakeside town of Bregenz, featuring opera and music recitals. It is perhaps ironic that Konstanz is the birthplace of Count Ferdinand von Zeppelin, constructor of the iconic airships, now used mainly as aerial billboards. Oh the humanity, indeed.

Back on Craig, I wander the suburban backstreets, looking for the ferry to Meersburg. After a pleasant ramble, I finally stumble upon the pier. I'm expecting a long queue of cars and passengers on this public holiday. Instead, I'm immediately waved on board a waiting ferry by a uniformed ticket seller who directs me and Craig to the starboard side, away from the fast loading vehicles. Within a few minutes, the lines are drawn and we're underway. I buy a reasonably priced ticket from the same gentleman and enjoy the thrill of crossing a narrow passage of the Bodensee. Craig and I salute German efficiency as we revel in the excitement of an, albeit brief, ferry journey.

Meersburg is a medieval town with a castle dating from the 7th Century. The town rises steeply from the lake and is divided into two sections, upper and lower, both free of cars. We disembark in a shaky clatter of gangplanks and gritted teeth, before cycling at snail's pace along the pedestrian promenade on the lake's edge. With the teeming throng, it's not really the place for a bicycle with panniers, but I have no choice. My haphazard directions to the hotel indicate I have to follow the lake for a kilometre before turning left.

I look left.

It's a very steep hill, just past the two superb buildings of heavy crossbeam timber and pastel colours atop a sharply-sloping vineyard. I change to granny gear and set myself the onerous task of climbing this hill as quickly as possible. Once on top, I ask for directions to my hotel and am sent along a busy road, full of BMWs and Mercedes, all looking for a parking space. My hotel is near a noisy intersection at the entrance to the upper town. Perfect.

The friendly man at reception shows me my room - my extremely small room, barely large enough for a single bed and my panniers. In this tourist-rich town, it is very cheap and in a good location, so after leaving Craig in the sunny but secure garden I wander into town.

I stroll through the imposing old archway and join the milling throng in a tourist daze, gawking at the variety and quantity of food on offer. Oh yeah, and the castle, the lovely town square of cobblestones, the multitude of cafes, the huge wooden water wheel, the wonderfully preserved wooden crossbeam houses and the intricate paintings on many of the public buildings. Meersburg wears its history and artifice with the aplomb of an elegant courtesan - forever welcoming, yet discreetly aloof and impenetrable.

I sit outdoors at a lakeside restaurant and order a beer from a dark-haired waitress with a fine array of tattoos on her arms and torso. Yes, she is wearing a rather revealing outfit.

This is the view in front of me. A bottle of beer, a line of stunted oak trees, flower boxes on the fence protecting the crowds from falling off the promenade, the turquoise lake five kilometres wide at this point with every type of water craft - yachts, beautiful wooden power boats, dinghys, kayaks, ferries and old steamers - all crisscrossing the water as if in a choreographed dance and in the distance the Swiss shoreline and hills rising behind. If I turn my head just a little to the left, why there's the Swiss Alps, still patched in snow despite the Spring weather. It's a wonderful scene, if only all the people would get out of the way!

A woman walks past with an ice-cream cone the size of an Olympic torch. She holds it aloft and takes a huge bite. Three steroid-enhanced men in tight t-shirts and designer sunglasses walk behind her with a swagger. I shudder and order a warm apple strudel just to prolong my time at the cafe, of course.

The man at the next table eats a huge cherry pie, washed down with a giant glass of Coca-cola and a coffee. His wife picks disinterestedly at her cheesecake. She pushes it away, half-finished. Her partner picks up the spoon and quickly scoffs it. At the other table, four people eat schnitzels the size of feet, accompanied by noodles, chips and a salad. The amount of food we eat is disgus ... oh sorry, here comes my strudel.

In the evening, the town quietens noticeably as the day-trippers all head home. I sit in the village square and admire the sheer dour grey walls of the castle. After a hearty risotto in an Italian restaurant, I wander back down to the lake. On the village pier is a curious sculpture by our friend Peter Lenk who designed Imperia at Konstanz. This piece is a tall mast with numerous playful figures attached. Each of the figures depicts someone who has figured prominently in the history of Meersburg. Cheekily, he has cast the famous poet Annette von Droste-Hulshoff as a seagull and the hunchbacked spinster Wendelgart as a big-breasted wine wench. It's an enchanting and humourous work that lives up to its name of Magische Saule (Magic Column).

Accommodation: Hotel Viktoria, Stefan Lochner Street 1, Meersburg. Budget choice hotel very close to the old town, with friendly staff, secure space for bicycles, wifi and a wholesome breakfast. Rooms can be small and if on the road side of the building could be noise affected. My score: 12/20

Restaurant: Meersburg has a smorgasbord of restaurants along the promenade or on the steep but fun-filled Steigstrasse. My suggestions are an Italian Restaurant on Steigstrasse (sorry, forgotten the name!) with outdoor tables in a courtyard, or the more expensive Aurichs Weinbar/Restaurant at Steigstrasse 28, which has lovely views of the lake from the terrace. Or take your chances along the promenade where you'll pay more for the privilege of people-watching and enjoying the lakeside breeze.

Route tips: Konstanz is worth a half-day cycle along the foreshore and through the historic city centre. Don't miss Meersburg. It is one of the jewels on the lake.

Distance cycled today: 51 km

Actual distance: 48 km

What I should have said: 'Fraulein, your tattoos are an art gallery for we beer lovers.'

Chapter Four:

Meersburg to Lindau and return

After a tasty breakfast, I've left the great weight of my panniers in the hotel room and set out on Craig with only the great weight of last night's dinner to lug around. Craig and I both notice the difference, the creaks in his suspension and my knees have disappeared as we cycle past palatial houses with immaculate gardens and expansive views of Lake Constance, or Bodensee as the Germans know it.

Old grapevines tangle up and over wooden sheds while apple trees bear fruit early in the season in neatly-rowed and netted orchards. Stalls beside the bike path sell buckets of apples and bottles of apple juice.

In Hagnau am Bodensee, the Rathaus has a flowering garden leading down to the shore and we cyclists have the privilege of riding straight under the imposingly wide and regal building through a convenient tunnel. I admire a town hall that is so approachable. Next to the path, in the garden is a small amphitheatre for musical recitals.

It's another fine sunny day, thankfully with less tourist traffic than yesterday's madness. Craig and I cruise along at a slow pace, humming a tune, admiring the sparkling water of the lake, the trilling of birds, the thwack thwack thwack of me trying to change into the correct gear. Must get that serviced soon. One good shove and yep, all is silent again.

'What say we stop for lunch, Craig old man?'

And sure enough up ahead, a beer garden nestles under trellised vines where scores of cyclists lounge on bench seats, all enjoying a beer. The cafe is rather canteen-like, with cheery middle-aged waitresses serving schnitzels and chips with gravy or bratwurst rolls to a long line of eager diners.

Everyone eating at a table is a cyclist. Families on a leisurely day out, old men riding home from the shop, couples in matching cut-off beige-coloured pants, the road-warrior lycra brigade and one very hungry Australian. Perhaps it's impossible to cycle past without being drawn into the inviting garden? And I must say the beer is impossibly cheap - a bottle of water costs more than the refreshing amber fluid. So I partake.

After lunch, I am overtaken by a posse of rampaging camping cyclists, each carrying enough equipment for a round-the-world tour. They have panniers front and back, but some even pull fully-loaded trailers behind their bikes as well as shouldering bulging backpacks. They struggle uphill in a fug of sweat and grunting before tearing downhill at a frightening pace. I'm expecting to come around the next corner and find enough camping gear strewn across the path to satisfy a lost squadron of boy scouts.

The obsession with taking large quantities of baggage has always intrigued me. My wife and I visit Europe from Australia for three months every year and never bring more than one carry-on bag each. Although Craig may complain about our weight, I have crossed all of France with two mid-size rear panniers and a small backpack for my laptop. I have never felt short of clothes. Admittedly, I am not camping but surely the addition of a tent doesn't require two extra panniers and a bike trailer?

I suppose if one is planning to camp out regularly, the addition of a portable stove and a saucepan and food is necessary. But one of the paramount joys of visiting a country is eating at the local restaurants and witnessing not only the changing cuisine but the social life that flourishes in each region. I understand my budget may seem extravagant, but I'm always amazed at how cheap local restaurants and hotels can be once away from the tourist traps.

I admire the hearty and resourceful campers, more power to them. But a warm shower, a glass of beer and a leisurely few hours in the evening eating my fill at a village restaurant cannot be surpassed in my humble opinion.

Just before Lindau, I come across a bicycle coffee van parked under a shade tree. I stop to have an espresso and admire the vehicle. It's an extended three-wheeler that comes complete, when unpacked, with a full-sized espresso machine, an umbrella, a few deckchairs and a charming barista wearing a beret and three-quarter length apron. We sip our coffees and admire the view. Correction, he admires the view, I wonder how I can encourage him to let me have a spin on his bicycle?

Lindau is a Bavarian town linked to a small island of the same name, very close to the Austrian border. Just across the harbour are the green Austrian hills. And if I turn south-west, there in the haze of the afternoon are the snow-capped Swiss Alps. It's a perfect location for a town and Lindau ramps up the charm factor by displaying the famous Bayerische Lowe - the Bavarian Lion - a six metre high sculpture carved from local marble, sitting on a plinth guarding the entrance to the small harbour. Opposite the Lion is Bavaria's only lighthouse. And gazing at both landmarks are thousands of tourists in the cafes strung along the promenade. After tethering Craig to a bicycle hitching post, I choose a fine looking establishment with a raised and sheltered verandah at the front and take a seat before ordering a beer. It's hard to pass up the opportunity to look at three countries at the same time. Actually, Liechtenstein is only a few kilometres away as well. Feasibly I could cycle in four countries in the one afternoon ... but I have another beer instead. Tax havens masquerading as Principalities are not my cup of tea or jug of beer, as it were.

Curiously, there is no binding agreement between the countries sharing the lake as to where the border lies. Switzerland believes the border should be drawn in the middle of the lake. Typically Swiss. The other two countries have ambiguous opinions.

The lake and its easy climate have attracted civilisations for thousands of years beginning with the Stone Age weavers and fishermen. If I'm forced to survive with my hands, I cannot think of a more pleasant location, sitting on the shore looking out over this lovely expanse of water, the high clouds floating past, a fish dangling from the end of my line.

At the table next to me are four men in their mid-fifties. They are all eating dessert. Two devour large portions of strudel covered in cream, the other two are enjoying cheesecakes. They wash down these sizeable treats with large glasses of beer and smaller cups of coffee. Caffeine, sugar and alcohol, a strange combination. The largest man of the four, wearing a bulging Brazilian football jersey, moves his chair away from the table as if trying to put more distance between himself and the treats on offer. He surveys the mass of empty plates on the table, no doubt wondering where all the food went. I'm tempted to join them and order an enticing cheesecake but I have a rather long cycle back to Meersburg and I doubt my legs can pull any more weight.

I untether Craig from his leash and we walk around the narrow alleys of the old town. The Altes Rathaus - the old town hall - is perhaps Lindau's finest building, dating from the 15th century and given an elegant facelift one hundred and fifty years later. The fresco and steepled roof give it a much more modern appearance than its age suggests.

Reluctantly, I jump back on Craig and cycle slowly along the lake shore back to Meersburg. It's a very relaxed journey, stopping frequently for water breaks and photo opportunities of yet another Swiss Alp rising from the distant shoreline. By the time I'm back at the Viktoria Hotel and Craig is resting in his garden, it's time for dinner and more beer. I wonder if the waitress has added another tattoo?

Accommodation: Hotel Viktoria, Stefan Lochner Street 1, Meersburg. Budget choice hotel very close to old town, with friendly staff, secure space for bicycles, wifi and good breakfast. Rooms can be small and if on the road-side of the building could be noise affected. My score: 12/20

Route tips: Lake Constance is the perfect location for a week of leisurely cycling. Where else can you visit four countries so easily. Meersburg and Lindau are excellent bases for forays into Switzerland and Austria. A train runs between the two towns and ferries cross the lake, linking various major towns.

Distance cycled today: 82 km

Actual distance: 80 km

What I should have said: 'Would you like to swap bicycles, sir? Your coffee cart for my sleek red beauty?'

Chapter Five:

Meersburg to Sigmaringen, Germany

On another clear sky day, I finally take my leave of lovely Meersburg and with Craig fully-loaded once again, cycle along the lake in the opposite direction to yesterday towards Uberlingen. The path wanders between the lake and a secondary road with large houses hugging the foreshore and vineyards carpeting the gentle slopes. The water is jade green and shallow this far up the lake. A man sitting in a giant plastic strawberry catches my attention, as do the luscious red berries he's selling. I buy a punnet, sit at a bus stop and eat half of them. The juice dribbles down my chin. A bus pulls up at my stop, mistaking me for a passenger not a gourmand! I smile at the driver and point to my bike. He gives a friendly wave and pulls out onto the busy road. After wrapping the remaining berries under clothes to hopefully prevent them getting too warm, I continue my cycle alternating between the traffic-filled road and the footpath.

I'm so lost in the memory of the strawberries that I fail to notice I've ridden past the end of the lake. I look back in vain to wave goodbye. As Homer Simpson, the great American philosopher and nuclear technician would say, 'Yuuuummmm, strawberries.'

Today I'm hoping to rejoin the Euro Velo 6 route along the famous Danube River. But I don't have a map and so I'm planning to town-hop until I reach the path. Or get stranded in a forest and survive on strawberries until I'm found by a German lumberjack team.

A kind soul has installed bird houses thirty metres up a cliff face. His handiwork is well used, judging by the flapping and squawking and babybird-heads-poking-out! The road climbs gradually for the next hour. I can't locate a bike path so I brave the road. Trucks are as courteous as pensioners at a bowls club, all waiting their turn, no hurry Dear.

I have no idea where I am, so let's call this Bodensee Heights, shall we? Acres of wheat fields and cheery orchards - sorry, that should read cherry orchards - grow either side of the highway. I see a sign with a bicycle symbol pointing into the forest, so having no better idea I gleefully pedal onto the wide path. Away from the road it's very quiet. A few birds, a distant rumble of an aeroplane and the creak of Craig's suspension. It's very pleasant but with the thick tree cover I have no idea in which direction I'm heading. In boy scout mode, I look up at the sun. Uuummm, maybe I'm heading west? Or north? There's nothing to do but suck it in and pedal faster, hoping I'll reach another sign.

The path gets smaller, bumpier and less used as the forest envelops me. I haven't seen another cyclist or bushwalker and I'm desperately hoping I don't come to a t-junction as I have no idea which way I should turn. Usually at this point, I start having vivid daydreams of raging storms, wild boars and rearing snakes. Such is the imagination of a city-bound cyclist, more at home in traffic-clogged streets than in a lonely forest.

Suddenly, the enveloping trees part and I'm cycling through open fields of wheat with a bruised sky of dark cloud on the horizon. The bike path joins a rambling country lane that I imagine will eventually lead me to a village.

Ten minutes later, I enter the perfect German hamlet with an old church of muscular dimensions next to a school in a stone building, opposite a cow barn covered in solar panels opening out onto a green pasture leading down to a bridge over a bubbling stream. Next to the creek is a football field with the nets still attached to both goals, patiently waiting for Saturday morning. In the backyard of one house a family eat lunch. The smell of bratwurst wafts across the hedge where I cruise enviously past.

I stop for lunch in Messkirch, a town of crossbeam timber houses and a plain white Renaissance castle dating from the 16th century. The local delicatessen serves tasty warm bratwurst on a roll for three Euro. At the crossroads, I consult the regional map and plot a route towards the Danube - straight ahead to Engelwies, right to Vilsingen and so on.

Route 313 is a quiet road that meanders between wheat fields and forest. The storm clouds have drifted north so I relax and dawdle the afternoon away. In a small village atop a hill, I come across a teenage boy riding his bike. I ask him the way to the Danube. He does not speak English and my German attempt at pronouncing 'Donau' is obviously so poor, he has no idea what I want. I cannot think of a good way to mime the word 'river', so I keep repeating various pronunciations of Donau. Eventually, he either understands I'm after the river or just decides to send me down a backroad in order to be free of the raving lunatic. I bow and say, 'danke.' He quickly rides off in the opposite direction as I excitedly plunge down a hill towards a clump of trees. Downhill. Trees. It must be ...

The first sight of the mighty Danube is anti-climatic. It is shallow, very narrow and hardly the river of romance - more a creek of dragonflies and weeds.

It will be my frequent companion for the next one thousand kilometres. When it comes to rivers that have enchanted me, the Danube is up there with the Mississippi. I've ridden beside the Mississippi near the delta at New Orleans and although it was twenty-six years ago, I vividly recall the disappointment of cycling alongside an imposing levee bank that obstructed my view of Old Man River. I'd ride up the grass embankment every kilometre to sneak a peek at the mighty waterway, wide and slow, before slinking back down to the bumpy tarmac.

The juvenile Danube does not need a levee. It's hardly the Blue Danube up here, near the source. In fact, it's so shallow and insignificant, I see two children wading mid-stream a few kilometres before Sigmaringen. Their father sleeps in the grass on the bank, certain his children cannot drown in such a piddling stream. But it is the Danube, the second-longest river in Europe and a waterway that acts as a border for ten countries. The Euro Velo 6 now follows the Danube all the way to the delta in Romania.

To celebrate my meeting with the Danube, I eat the last of my strawberries and admire the fish ladders constructed to allow migration upstream. My destination tonight is Sigmaringen, a pretty town with a monster castle. Bleak, overbearing and austere, the medieval Sigmaringen Castle was briefly the seat of the French Vichy Government-in-exile at the end of World War Two. Perhaps that colours its appearance for me. To lighten my mood, at the foot of this pile of rock, I eat rhubarb strudel outside a backerei and contemplate tomorrow's waltz along the Danube. Ouch!

My hotel is located a kilometre from town along a cycle path leading me over the river and past a scar of modern supermarket developments with over-sized car parks and billboards advertising toilet paper and Coca-cola. At night, I wander back into town and eat in a trendy bar-restaurant with young waitresses dressed in vogue black offering excellent pastas and pizza.

I walk back to the hotel in the twilight with the brooding castle rearing above the Danube. I'm exhausted but can't resist turning on the television in my hotel room and delighting in the awfulness of soap operas and game shows, all inhabited by people who speak a language I can't understand. The pretty blond woman appears to be having trouble with her dark and mysterious boyfriend while the middle-aged married couple are considering a divorce or arguing over something in the garden. I can't tell which. They shout and point outside. Either one of them is leaving or he hasn't bothered to mow the lawn in weeks. I end the dispute with the remote and fall asleep.

Accommodation: Jagerhof Hotel, Hauptstrasse 223, Weibersbrunn. Quiet hotel in a suburb of Sigmaringen. Garage for the bicycle, comfortable rooms with a balcony, wifi costs extra. My score: 12/20.

Route tips: There's no clearly defined cycle route between these two towns and there will be a big hill somewhere along the way, no matter which road you take. Wander at leisure though, as the distance back to the Danube isn't huge. Perhaps the best suggestion would be the slightly longer cycle back to Tuttlingen and follow the Danube from there, allowing you the opportunity to experience the gorge.

Distance cycled today: 72 km

Actual distance: 65 km

What I should have said: 'How long do you sit inside the strawberry each day?'

Chapter Six:

Sigmaringen to Ulm, Germany

For the first time on this trip, the day dawns cloudy and grey with the threat of rain. This is excuse enough for a large breakfast of the usual Germanic treats - cheese, dark bread, ham, eggs, the misplaced tart or three. Although Uncle Google tells me the expected distance today is eighty kilometres, with the twisting and turning young Danube, I'm sure it will be much longer. What say one more apricot tart?

Craig greets me with a cursory shrug, something about the smell of this stuffy garage overnight. I give him a gentle pat on the crossbar and pedal slowly downhill to join the Danube path. We both offer a cursory goodbye to the gloomy Sigmaringen Castle as we cycle on a bridge over the train tracks. An occasional commuter cyclist greets me as I keep to the right side of the Danube. Once outside of town, the river meanders sluggishly through a wide valley of farms and a series of small villages with plain houses, usually surrounding a stocky white-painted church. In the square of each hamlet, the traditional maypole has been erected. I'm too late for the fete that takes place, either on May 1st or at the Pentecost but the decorations give each village a jaunty *we've just had a party* appeal. Near the maypole there's usually a temporary statue of a stork, often painted in outlandishly bright colours or in the case of one extravagant village, wearing a top hat and tails. If I was a self-respecting stork, I wouldn't be nesting in that town.

But there is an early migrant nesting in Zell. Judging by this rooftop, storks not only bring good luck but also a lovely frosting of bird droppings to colour the tiles. The tell-tale long neck pokes out from the twigs and appears to wish Craig and I a good day. I wave at the bird, in response. An oncoming motorist waves back, no doubt impressed with the friendliness of cyclists in this region.

Perhaps it's the low cloud and chilly temperature, but the day has a lonely desolate feel to it. Fields of rape and wheat huddle close to the river, the forested hills are quiet, even the roads seem unusually devoid of traffic.

Only one way to break the prevailing mood ... buy a cake!

I spy a church steeple ahead and hope it's accompanied by a backerei in the village square. Craig and I pick up the pace. We're in luck! I'm greeted by a stout woman wearing a purple apron and a welcoming expression. My type of baker. I choose a slice of pastry - hard crust, jam-filled, topped with a buttery crumble. I'm too preoccupied slavering over this treat to get its German name. Let's call it a *bewolkten tag kuchen*? Which loosely translates as *cloudy day cake*.

Back in the saddle, the valley narrows and the path starts to climb significantly. With all the extra weight of cake, I struggle to the crest of a hill and rest under a lone tree. Opposite is an elegant white church with apricot trim and a domed steeple. In the distance, fields of low wheat stretch along the plateau punctuated by an occasional patch of forest. A lone songbird provides the accompanying soundtrack. I take a long satisfied swig of water and consider curling up on this seat like an old hobo, dozing in the soft noonday light.

After another hour of lazy cycling, I pull into Ehingen where the main square is decorated with a very tall maypole rising out of a fountain. Muscular office buildings line the cobblestone mall and I relax at an outdoor seat of a chain restaurant. I'm not particularly hungry so I order a serve of fries. The waitress looks almost as embarrassed as I am. But on this chilly dull day, I feel like starch and salt. The shoestring pile I'm offered threatens to topple off the large dinner plate. Oh dear. I eat as many as I can and slink away after paying my bill. Two euro to the cheap Australian riding the attractive red bicycle.

As if to punish me for my stinginess, it starts to rain a few kilometres outside of Ehingen. I shrug into my rain poncho which also covers my backpack, so I look like a helmeted hunchback set free from the Cathedral. I could certainly use sanctuary at present as the rain falls steadily. The path leads beside a tree-lined Danube, with water-lillies dotting the shallow water near the bank. The spray from the path soaks my shoes, despite wearing shoe covers. I pull the jacket hood over my helmet and plough onwards. Another church on a hill, another cow barn covered in solar panels, another stork perescoping from an oversized nest, another rain cloud following the lone cyclist. Eventually in the late afternoon after one hundred and five kilometres, I reach Ulm.

Of course, a few kilometres before entering the town, I can see the world's largest church steeple guiding me into the city centre. Indeed, the Ulm Munster Church is a monster with a steeple 161 metres high. The square in front of the church is empty, all the cafes pushed well back so visitors can take in the enormity of the steeple's loft. It's neither elegant or particularly attractive but I love the Gothic spires, the massive organ and the haunting sculpture of Jeremiah. I decline climbing the 768 steps to reach the pinnacle. Instead I play the humourous game of trying to photograph the complete church. This requires the clumsy Australian to walk backwards while looking into the viewfinder of his camera. One more step should ... oops, excuse me, dear fraulein. Yep, it's a very tall steeple.

Next to the Cathedral is the Rathaus adorned with a series of vivid paintings on each outer wall, accompanied by a story which unfortunately I can't translate. In each painting someone is pointing a finger at someone else. Methinks there's a cautionary tale being told. Regardless, it's a lovely way to decorate a town hall.

I haven't pre-booked a hotel so Craig and I wander the streets looking for a cheap room. We wander for quite a while until I find one right next to the church, surprisingly. The cheery owner who speaks excellent English shows me my small but comfortable room. He assures me Craig will be happy in the basement. As we're talking the Church bells starts chiming at five pm. A thought crosses my mind.

'Does the bell chime at every hour?' I ask.

The owner smiles grimly, 'Every hour, all night.'

'All night,' I repeat, perhaps taking in the enormity of one hundred and five kilometres of cycling followed by an interrupted night's sleep.

The owner nods wearily, holding up his hands in a way that says, there is nothing to be done.

I sigh.

To celebrate my arrival in ding-dong town, I walk to a trendy cafe where an attractive young woman with a ponytail, green apron and an intricate tattoo lacing her bicep serves me an excellent cafe macchiato and teaches me how to ask for tap water in German.

'Leitungswasser,' I repeat until the bill arrives. I give her a tip for German lessons.

In the early evening, I wander the streets of a busy and crowded Ulm. There are many young people sitting in pubs or cafes, wandering the malls, talking in groups outside fashion stores. The University of Ulm, established in 1967 has obviously benefitted the town both economically and by lowering the median age of the population considerably.

Ulm, like many cities with a river flowing through it, has a 'Venice quarter.' My hotel manager implored me to check it out. It's not the enchanted city, but it is lovely, particularly the 16th Century small hotel built over a stream, which looks in danger of sinking. It's called, appropriately, Schiefes Haus - the crooked house. To stay a night in this hotel only costs twice as much as every other lodging in the area, such is the novelty of the lean. I wonder if each bed tilts up, down, or sideways?

Time for dinner.

After the fries fiasco of lunch, I'm determined to treat myself to some hearty fare. I take an inordinately long time to choose a restaurant, wandering up and down narrow alleys, reading menus as best I can. What is a Kasseler Rippchen? And can I have it without chips? Finally, I decide on Basil's Restaurant. It's elegant and stately, despite the name. An immaculately dressed waiter leads me to my table.

I sit in a leather seat with wide armrests, perusing a menu of Greek delights from Giros to Fisherman's Plate while admiring the white tablecloth, the hanging chandeliers, dark wood trim and ornamental Greek Doric column. The waiter kindly lights a candle on my table and brings a plate of olives and crispy bread. I order a pils beer and lean back in my cushy chair, satisfied.

And then 'Nights in White Satin' comes on the sound system.

Despite this, the meal is fantastic. A bowl of 'Farmers Salad' arrives first - tomatoes, cucumbers, onion, capsicum and feta cheese. It's substantial enough to feed a flotilla of famished farmers but I scoff the lot. The main course is a plate of grilled meat - pork chop, lamb cutlet, chicken breast, a mince pattie resembling a flattened kofta and slices of crunchy giro, accompanied by a bowl of potatoes and a wash of zingy tzatziki. It's delicious and ridiculously cheap at Euro 15. I order another beer and count my good fortune.

And then they play 'Nights in White Satin' again!

To make up for this, the lovely waiter brings me a complimentary glass of Ouzo. Aaahhh.

Tomorrow, my wife arrives and we begin our cycle down the

Danube together. I am enormously excited. The church bells ring, as if to remind me of the joys of marriage.

Accommodation: Hotel Zum Anker, Rabengasse 2, Ulm. Friendly English-speaking hosts, small comfortable rooms, free wifi, good breakfast. If you're a light sleeper, you may want to get a hotel further away from the hourly bells of Munster Cathedral. My score: 12/20.

Restaurant: Basil's Grill-Restaurant, Platgasse 20, Ulm. I implore you to take your leave of schnitzels and go to Basil's. Despite the name and the dubious soundtrack, it is fine dining at a budget price. Servings are huge and delicious and the salad fresh and healthy and devoid of the usual creamy overwrought German dressing. 17/20

Route tips: While it's a considerable distance for a single day of cycling, I'd still recommend staying consecutive nights in Sigmaringen and Ulm, both lovely towns with good restaurants. The day of cycling is through enchanting and quiet villages amid scenic farmland. Nothing spectacular, but relaxing and rewarding.

Distance cycled today: 105 km

Actual distance: 82 km

What I should have said: 'The bells, the bells, no more of the bells!'

Chapter Seven:

Ulm to Lauingen, Germany

This morning dawns cloudy and cold. After a substantial German breakfast of yoghurt, ham, cheese, fruit and a basket of sturdy bread, I eagerly await the arrival of my wife.

Today, I begin the second part of my Danube cycle, happily with Cathie alongside me.

The birds sing louder, the swans elegantly glide along beside us and the fields of rape blush with spring colour, all because I am no longer alone. I reach for Cathie's hand and nearly lead us both into a watery ditch. We decide to ride single file, just in case.

Craig is particularly chirpy this morning, perhaps excited to have a cycling companion, appropriately named Jenny. Jenny is a petite grey and black bicycle of alluring curves and a jaunty disposition. This is Cathie's first long-distance cycle and she nervously plots her way along the path, listening to my seemingly endless tales of food, fields and freedom offered by the bicycle.

A few kilometres outside of Ulm we catch up to a German couple who look to be doing some serious touring. They wear expensive goretex jackets and rain trousers and each ride a sturdy bicycle power-assisted by batteries. Their substantial amount of gear is safely packed in waterproof black panniers. The man has a map attached to his handlebar bag. All four of us stop at an intersection, with the signs offering a confusing array of possibilities. The man consults his map and shrugs. We tentatively cycle along the left track until we come upon a gentleman walking his dog. Our map reader confidently asks him the way to Gunzburg, or at least I assume that's what he's asking as neither Cathie or I are fluent in German.

The man issues a volley of complicated instructions while his dog waits patiently, smiling benignly. Voices are raised and fingers point in various directions. I get the impression there's a disagreement as to the best route to take. Finally we all cycle off, only to join a line of cars waiting at a railway crossing. Our leader leans close to a car window and mimes a question about directions. The old lady smiles and points the way we're all facing. The train passes and we turn left, then right before becoming lost again.

A volley of what I imagine are German expletives fills the morning air and four people look in each direction for appropriate signs. Our leader, who I've christened Livingstone for obvious reasons, decides to backtrack. His wife, a tall imposing woman with short hair and a shy demeanour smiles patiently. We have little option but to follow him. After a few minutes we arrive in Thalfingen and, sure enough, there's a sign pointing us in the correct direction. I take this opportunity to bid farewell to our friends while we all admire the village church, painted pink and white. Around the corner is a backerei. I consult my watch.

'Any time is good enough for cake,' says Cathie, reading my thoughts, as usual. I have missed her more than I can say.

The woman behind the counter allows us to point and smile as compensation for speaking German with all the skill of a shy three-year-old. She wears a neat white smock and has a bakers hat, tilted at a jaunty angle. She appears to be the type of Grandmother who'd indulge the children with lots of cakes and treats. She nods at our choices.

I scoff a strawberry danish while Cathie delicately picks at a hazelnut strudel.

'Will we eat lunch in Gunzburg?' she asks.

'It's 9:45 and we've just eaten cake,' I say.

'What's your point,' she responds. We both grin, glad to be together and talking about our favourite subject.

Back on the bikes, we are soon on a logging track cycling through a forest of tall trees with piles of logs stacked high every fifty metres. The Danube slowly drifts beside us. Ahead is a young couple, each cycling with a trailer attached. In the woman's trailer is a tent and plastic bags which I imagine are full of clothes. In the other trailer is a child, perhaps two year old, sitting up and surveying the world rolling past him at 15 kph. We offer a little wave. The proud Dad grins.

Sunshine filters through the tree canopy and I remember the weather forecast - gloomy predictions of showers all day and the temperature struggling to pass 10 degrees. I consider removing my jacket but refuse to tempt the weather gods. I also leave my sunglasses in the backpack. As we cruised out of Ulm this morning, I was tempted to put them on but knew that as soon as I did the predicted rain would arrive. So they're staying packed away and the rain will not dare to fall.

Such are the superstitions of a long-distance-cyclist.

Leipheim is an attractive town on the right side of the Danube with a white-washed church, a museum that looks as if it could have been designed by a child, houses with verdant gardens and a van dispensing grilled chicken at a reasonable price. A robust old man strides purposefully up the hill to the van and keenly surveys the rotating birds, turning crispy brown. He orders two. We restrain ourselves, despite the lingering aroma.

I smile at the apparent wealth and comfort, remembering a story I'd read about the town. In the early 19th Century following the Napoleonic Wars, the folk of Leipheim endured many years of hardship and famine. The people prayed for a good harvest and when one arrived, duly celebrated by holding a huge celebration they called a Kinderfest. The tradition continues in June every year when the happy citizens of Leipheim hold a *celebration of the children,* which includes songs and dance and the obligatory beer festival. I liked that very much. On the bridge across the Danube there's a statue of a man holding a child aloft, perhaps to show the gods that the people of this town have kept their promise.

The next town of Gunzburg has a far more sinister recent past, being the birthplace Josef Mengele, the Nazi medical officer at Auschwitz concentration camp. Mengele fled to South America at the end of the Second World War. In 1970, his father died and there were widespread rumours that the evil doctor had returned from his exile to attend the funeral. Despite official denials, the citizens of Gunzburg were accused of harbouring one of the most wanted men in the Nazi regime. Later research proved the suspicions to be ill-founded. But a stigma hung over the town for years afterwards.

Despite this, Gunzburg is a lovely town set on a hill with enticing archways as entry points to the old town. I inadvertently choose the steepest cobblestone road to ride up and we both enter the main square sweating and puffing heavily. But after a long morning meandering along forest paths and riverside tracks, it's time for lunch!

After a fine meal of spaghetti for me and salad for Cathie, we relax at the table and my wife surveying the bucolic scene says, 'I can't imagine what this town must have been like during the war.'

A minute later, a bell tolls loudly above our heads and four fighter jets thunder past. We look at each other and decide not to mention the war again.

We wander the long rectangular old square. It's busy at noon with cafes and beirgartens beside fashion stores all vying for the attention of the pedestrians. At one end of the square, a man attempts to reverse park a Ferrari behind a Porsche while a motorist in a black Mercedes looks on. We cyclists avoid the bling-fest and leave our more sedate modes of transport unlocked outside a church. I confidently walk to the imposing wooden door and turn the handle. Nothing happens. I push hard against the door. Still no movement. I try the handle once more. Damn.

Cathie steps forward and easily pulls the door open. I hadn't thought of that.

All embarrassment is quickly forgotten as we step inside. This is one glorious interior. Cherubs hang from every wall, painted murals - pink, blue, apricot and white - appear to be glowing. There's more gold-braid than at a Liberace concert. It's all eye-poppingly over the top, yet the church loses none of its sacredness or quiet calm. Like the church at Bad Sackingen, I feel I've stepped inside some enchanting fairytale, a world of vivid colours, angels and smiling cherubs. I would love to attend a service here. I imagine the Minister would be a handsome smiling man, proud to be speaking in such radiant surroundings. I trust his sermon would be full of optimism and promise, not guilt and austerity.

Back on a logging path beside the Danube, I see three ducks who appear to be playing *hide and seek*. One duck sits in long grass, occasionally raising his elongated neck to see who's watching. The other two quack and waddle along the path in opposite directions, scanning the undergrowth. The hiding duck spies me and quickly ducks his head, if you'll pardon the pun.

We cycle into the outer suburbs of Lauingen in the early afternoon and to celebrate our arrival Cathie gets her first puncture of the trip. The sun comes out. I take off my jacket and get to work. Thirty minutes of swearing later, we're both back in the saddle and riding slowly into town looking for a cycle shop to buy a spare tube. There are three bike shops within five hundred metres. The sun keeps shining.

It's cappuccinos in the village square for afternoon tea and I heroically resist the tiramisu. Actually, that's not true. I asked for one, but they were all out of desserts. I issue a proud vow of abstinence ... until dinner. Opposite our cafe is the tower called the Schimmelturm, which has its origins in the 15th century, originally serving as a watch tower. Nowadays, it's the centre piece of an annual event called the *Hexentanz, or witches dance.* You guessed it, lots of locals dress up and dance and play elaborate games including my favourite where the winter witch is involved in a tug-of-war with the Spring fools. Of course the witch loses and the locals no doubt go back to dancing and drinking beer. I'd like to be here for that festival, but we're a little too early.

The hotel I've booked is very swank and we're greeted by a well-dressed man who shows us where to leave the bikes and happily carries our dirty panniers upstairs to the room. The first thing Cathie and I do is check the pillows. German hotels have an annoying habit of offering each person one square thin pillow, largely devoid of feathers. It's like laying your head on a cotton rag. This hotel, bless them, offers two pillows, full of duck down. Perhaps that's why the ducks were playing hide and seek?

Accommodation: Lodner Genieerhotel, Imhofstasse 7, Lauingen. Lovely hotel just around the corner from the town square and rathaus. Friendly staff, great breakfast, wifi costs E3 and there's a secure place for bicycles. My score: 16/20

Restaurant: Pizzeria Italia, Herzog-Georg Strasse, Lauingen. I had an excellent scallopini al vino bianco with well-cooked vegetables and a huge salad for the princely sum of E9.90. Good simple Italian food at a bargain price. Large serves, friendly staff, cold beer. My score: 15/20.

Route tips: Detour to Gunzburg which is only a kilometre from the Danube to enjoy the wonderful sensory overload of the Church of Our Lady, designed by the 17th century architect, Dominikus Zimmermann. The logging tracks beside the river are quiet and calming and feature accompanying birdsong and swanning ... swans.

Distance cycled today: 64 km

Actual distance: 60 km

What I should have said: 'I know church doors open outward in Bavaria, Cathie. I was just testing you.'

Chapter Eight:

Lauingen to Neuburg an der Donau, Germany

I open the hotel window at six-thirty in the morning and poke my head out. It's not raining. Me and the tabby cat on a window ledge opposite approve. He licks his paw while I retreat to the sanctuary of the breakfast room which is an elegant expanse of high ceilings and stonework. Pity none of the sturdy tables are prepared for diners at this early hour. The owner shrugs when we apologise for making him work so early and sets about offering us a spread of ham and cheese with knotty dark bread rolls and scrambled eggs and boiled eggs and bacon and muesli and yoghurt and orange juice and an espresso and yes, that should be sufficient, dear man.

We walk out ready to tackle a planned sixty-five kilometre cycle to Neuberg en der Donau. We roll downhill two hundred metres and immediately join a bike path beside the Danube which is looking splendidly quiet and peaceful this morning. A few joggers sweat past us and we wish them a 'gut morgen.' They appear too puffed to answer, nodding briskly instead. One day I'll understand the folly of running back and forward for an hour every morning, but not today as we veer off the river and enter another hard-dirt logging track. The birds start singing, the temperature chills a few degrees and I wax lyrical about the joys of cycling. Cathie stifles a yawn and when I look hurt, tries to pass it off as a lingering tiredness from yesterday's ride.

The logging track narrows and soon we are riding along a magical little path no wider than a metre with heavy forest either side. We bump across perfect little wooden bridges over cold streams and I almost expect to see fairies and elves cavorting among the trees. Instead I see Cathie steering daintily between two puddles without slowing down at all. I almost crash in my attempt at dodging the mud. Cathie suppresses a smirk.

A minute later the path opens out into a quiet park where a few locals are walking their dogs and letting them toilet where they want. This being efficient and tidy Germany, there is a pole with a plastic-bag dispenser for picking up after Rex.

Up a steep hill and we're already in Dillingen, a town of grey-painted imposing buildings lining the main street. Their bulk is offset by the planting of flowering trees all along the footpath. I'm admiring this street architecture and not looking where I'm going when I turn and face a man in a business suit. I veer left, he moves right. I do the opposite, he changes direction as we mirror each other's actions like some bad mime skit. We both laugh. He holds my wrist gently and pretends to move out of my way with elaborate evasion. I like Dillingen very much.

A few kilometres along the Danube at Hochstadt, Cathie and I agree that 9.15am is not too early for cake. The lady behind the counter offers me a delicious torte whose name I've forgotten but it had lots of the letters N and S and sounded like somebody was cleaning their nasal passages. Cathie chooses a nutty Danish and I apologise to all Danes for describing them as such. On display near the cash register is a sliced loaf of each of the breads the backerei sell. I count fourteen varieties as I'm paying the bill. I can't resist asking the lady if I can take a photo of her bread. She smiles indulgently, obviously convinced that Australia is such an impoverished country that its citizens go bonkers at the sight of bread.

The ride into Donauworth is fraught. We lose the bike path and instead join a posse of cars and trucks chasing us past strip shopping, McDonald's restaurants, $2 Discount stores and if you want to get your car serviced for forty-five Euros in Donauworth, I know just the place.

Donauworth was the site of one of the major incidents which led to the Thirty Years War in the 17th century. The town's Lutheran majority prevented the minority Catholics from holding a parade. One thing led to another and soon enough there was a riot and religious grievances which festered for another decade before the onset of three decades of bloodshed and retribution. Such is the beauty of religion.

When we do find the old town, the entrance is amusingly through a narrow tunnel with an elaborately decorated wall, which includes a lovely painting of a couple dressed in old-time farming clothes - he's wearing a jacket and neck-tie, she's carrying a basket which I suspect is full of freshly-picked strawberries. The town itself is just as sweet with pastel-coloured buildings and cobblestones and well-dressed citizens buying sturdy loaves of bread. No sign of hatred and upheaval this morning.

We enter a cafe and see the cycling couple from yesterday who helped us get lost so efficiently. They smile and pay the bill. Perhaps they're worried we're bad luck?

We both agree on ordering the Gulaschsuppe. On this cold bleak day, hot soup is just the treat. The waitress shakes her head when we ask for two servings and says something in German which I imagine means, 'My husband, who was supposed to cook the soup this morning instead got so drunk last night so all I can offer you is weiners.'

Flustered, we both nod. Weiners it is.

I'm not quite sure what goes into a weiner, but I imagine it's ground pork offcuts, mustard, paprika and a binding agent. For three Euro, Cathie and I have two each with brown bread and lots of mustard. It isn't a hearty soup.

The waitress picks up our empty plates and asks, 'Gut?'

I don't want to be rude, but for a moment I'm not sure how to answer. They were neither good nor bad. They were weiners. Cathie saves the day by using her best high school German to exclaim 'ser gut!' as if she'd just eaten a delicious five-course degustation meal. It's one reason I love her.

I'm sure she never lies to me though.

Full of weiner and hot air, we promptly ride the wrong way out of the old town and end up in the parking lot of the Euro Helicopter Company, which judging by the vehicles arrayed end to end is doing strong business. We back-track through the old town and head east, soon enough finding the ever-reliable green bike signs, pointing us towards Neuberg an der Donau along the historic and famous Romantik Strasse - the Romantic Road.

After three steep uphill climbs, each followed by a rollicking downhill, Cathie observes, 'I didn't realise romance had so many ups and downs.'

'That's because you're married to me,' I say.

Another hill appears on cue, and we both set ourselves to the task. And so begins an hour of joyous cycling. Yes, it's up and down, but the combination of a perfect tarmac for riding, expansive views back over wheat fields and the Danube and lovely villages each resplendent with a white-painted church, a maypole still festooned with decorations and stout houses with neat gardens, makes every climb worthwhile.

Graibach. Lechsend. Marxheim. None of these villages are on the tourist map, but each offers a slice of authentic rural Germany. A farmer drives his tractor full of hay into a barn. Another man cuts firewood with a mechanical wood splitter. A woman calls for her dog to come back when he looks too interested in chasing swallows. And two contented Australians smile romantically at one another.

After one long sweeping downhill, we find ourselves back on a dirt track atop a levee beside the Danube. The river has widened considerably while we've been romancing the road and it flows sluggishly in the mid-afternoon. Cathie rides ahead and I slow to enjoy the quiet.

Miraculously, we're joined by hundreds of swallows swooping low along the surface of the river and then banking sharply before heading straight for us on the levee. It's like a scene from a Hitchcock movie, only played for laughs not fear. Swallows have always been Cathie's favourite birds and here they are putting on a show for us. I'm amazed at how close they come. We cycle even slower to prolong the game but there are so many birds they appear happy to follow us all the way to the dam wall. We finally stop and they swoop away, no doubt to impress other cyclists with their superb aeronautical skills. Not to be outdone, a ballet of swans begins in the shallow water near the bank. Each bird ducks its head into water for ten seconds at a time, provocatively lifting its bottom towards us. It's a synchronised swimming demonstration.

We reluctantly cycle away from the Bird Circus on the Danube and into Neuberg en der Donau. We ride up a steep hill to the old town which in the mid-afternoon looks curiously deserted. The restaurants are closed and an occasional car slowly clatters over the cobblestones. Our hotel is a kilometre away in the new town.

Despite the early hour, the hotel owner, a woman with bad teeth and windswept hair welcomes us heartily and leads us upstairs to our room in the attic. The room is spotlessly clean and painted vivid white. It's at the end of a long corridor. Like the old town, this hotel seems deserted and lonely. I wonder if there are any other guests?

We change out of our lycra into casual clothes before walking along the main strasse towards the old town. The first shop we see has a wide variety of cakes decorating the window display. I peer through the window. There are no customers and no-one is behind the counter. We tentatively enter. A bell rings above the door and an old woman with grey hair and wearing a bright pink apron rushes out from the kitchen. She greets us with a long sentence that we don't understand. I imagine it's something to do with the cool weather and us being her only customers in the past year or two?

We each point at our cake of choice. The woman, in halting English offers us coffee. We look confused. There is no coffee machine and nowhere to sit. The old woman smiles and elaborately opens the wood-pannelled door leading to another room full of tables and chairs. It's like entering Aunt Violet's lounge room in 1972, with acres of brown and beige furnishings, orange tablecloths and photos of a woman with long blonde hair wearing a sensible cardigan and holding an umbrella. Could it be our host when she was younger?

The old lady brings us coffee in a china pot, accompanied by huge slices of cheesecake. Her husband arrives home from work, carrying his briefcase. He seems surprised to find people in the cafe. He walks through to the kitchen for an afternoon snack of cake and tea, I imagine.

We walk off the calories wandering the old town which is still deserted. The Neuberg Castle is an impressive building erected in the 16th century and now housing a gallery of baroque paintings, but alas, is shut by the time we arrive. We make do with a visit to the late Renaissance Hofkirche, a church built in 1608. It's a splendidly proportioned and regal building, painted a prominent yellow with a gold-plated clock on the tower wall.

In the evening, we walk through the new town full of people wandering home from work or admiring the window displays or preparing for a evening in the many restaurants and pubs. We choose a restaurant overlooking the river and are ushered into a warm dining room with wide windows. The only other diners are the same couple from yesterday with the electric bikes and the propensity for getting lost. We all laugh in greeting. It appears as if we'll be following each other across Germany. The man raises his beer glass and offers us a silent toast.

Accommodation: Gasthof Bergbauer, Funfzehnerstrasse 11, Neuberg an der Donau. Friendly hosts, good breakfast, fast wifi, perhaps a little expensive. My score: 14/20

Restaurant: Mythos Restaurant, Elisenplatz 15, Neuburg an der Donau. Situated right beside the Danube, this Greek restaurant offers hearty and authentic cuisine and lots of it. We ordered the two-person Grill Special and were overwhelmed with three types of meat, delicious rice and a large Greek Salad. Good value and lovely setting. My score: 14/20.

Distance cycled today: 73 km

Actual distance: 65 km

What I should have said: 'That display of birds is hard to swallow...' (Perhaps not)

Chapter Nine:

Neuburg an der Donau to Neustadt an der Donau, Germany

I know I keep raving about the German breakfast, but I'm easily swayed by copious amounts of good food arrayed in front of me. This morning I'm even given five bottles of different juices to choose from.

'I'll take the 100% apple, danke.'

The host has also sliced fresh kiwi-fruit, strawberries, apples and pears into a delicious salad. And if that's not enough natural sweetness, she's added a berry compote and natural yoghurt.

After we've scoffed this delight, she brings a cute wicker basket of eggs to our table and says something in German. Cathie wisely nods yes. I shake my head. I've never been a fan of hard-boiled eggs. The woman walks off with the basket and returns a few minutes later with a plate of scrambled eggs, cooked to perfection. As she offers Cathie the plate, I make a sound similar to the whining of a hungry dog. Three minutes later, I am also indulging in scrambled eggs.

Cathie says, simply, 'Never refuse food.'

Substantially heavier than last night, we cross the Danube and follow the sign which unfortunately points up a rather steep hill to Ingolstadt. No matter. I have eaten scrambled eggs.

When I reach the top, I have a lovely view back toward Neuburg, the castle imposing and fortress-like above the river. The morning is spent pedalling gentle kilometres between fields of wheat, rape and lettuce. A kilometre off to our right, the row of trees indicate the river course but it seems as if the Euro Velo 6 authorities have decided that we should be kept at a safe distance. Atop the next hill, I see that on the far side of the river are chimneys of industry spewing smoke into the cloudy sky. Smart Euro Velo 6 folk.

In the small village of Bergheim, we cycle past an old lady with a glorious knot of grey hair pushing what looks like a home-made mechanical footpath sweeper. But what could she be sweeping? There are no leaves about.

Dirt? From the footpath?

A few hundred metres along the same strasse, a teenage girl with long hair and braces smiles as we pass. She is also sweeping the footpath with the more tried and true method of a broom. I try to recall if I've ever seen a teenager sweeping anything, much less a footpath?

Who are these mysterious street sweepers of Bergheim. And why is dirt their apparent enemy?

Onward to Ingolstadt, birthplace of the Bavarian Illuminati, a secret society founded in 1776 whose goals included attempting to eliminate superstition, prejudice and the domination of the Catholic Church in influencing government policy. They also supported the education of women and believed the fairer sex should be treated as intellectual equals. Now that's one secret society I'd like to join! One of the founders was Adam Weishaupt who was the first lay professor of canon law at the local university. Of course such radical rationalism was hardly popular at the time and Weishaupt lost his position in 1784 and fled Bavaria.

Ingolstadt is also the setting in Mary Shelley's famous novel *Frankenstein* where Victor creates his monster.

That's the thing about university towns - there's always someone with a bright idea. My brilliant idea for the morning is to accompany Cathie to a backerei for an excellent strawberry danish and coffee. I'm quite fond of the German danish - they are substantial, sweet and the berries are appealingly fresh. I consider having another, but Cathie, my intellectual equal counsels against it.

We cycle around the old town and marvel at the Herzogskasten (the old castle), the Church of Our Lady, the ironically named 15th Century New Castle and the artistically-splendid Rathaus, but find nothing quite as beautiful as intellectual equality and free thinking. I dip my helmet to Adam Weishaupt and cycle out of town, full of stomach and of spirit.

We rejoin the Danube on a hard-packed dirt trail and cruise quietly along, with one eye on the black cloud threatening the horizon. I notice we are being followed by a peloton of rain-jacket wearing senior citizens, each with sensible waterproof panniers and sit-up black Dutch bikes. We pass a man walking his dog and he says something that I imagine is, 'It looks like it's about to rain.' I nod, agreeably. A few metres later we run out of bike path. The man points to his left, indicating the preferred route. We do an embarrassed u-turn and cycle back to the turn-off. The peloton cruises past us, also going the wrong way. I use elaborate hand gestures trying to explain the situation but only instil a measure of fear in the ladies of the party. The men just think I'm stupid.

Back on the correct and elevated path, we wave animatedly at the peloton who've also been informed by the nice man with a dog that they should follow us.

It's good to be on the Danube again, even when the showers begin. The swallows return and perform a sequel to yesterday's Hitchcockian fantasy. On one side of the levee is a series of lagoons fed by a running stream, on the other the languid river. A pheasant noisily flaps across our path. A kilometre further on, a deer scampers between the trees, his jaunty gait an apt metaphor for how we both feel happily following the course of this beautiful river.

We settle into a rhythm of conversation, recalling the meals we most enjoyed from our Italian holiday a few years ago; arguing over the Top Five pizzas of all time; debating why the Germans smother every salad in so much cream; and whether the correct term for cream is sahne or schlag. I prefer the clout of onomatopoeia in schlag.

A few kilometres further on, Cathie points to a peloton of cyclists on the opposite side of the Danube.

'Aren't they ...' she says.

I quickly turn and see that the path behind is clear. There was a bridge a kilometre back I vaguely remember riding under.

'Do you suppose we should ...' Cathie suggests.

'Nah. This looks fine,' I say.

Sure enough, the track runs out at the next bend in the river. Mercifully, there is a dam wall to ride across. We meekly follow the peloton of old, but wise people into Vohburg, a lovely village with distinctive entry gates and an old schloss and cemetery atop the hill. On this chilly Saturday, a couple about to be married are getting romantic wedding photos taken with the background of the Danube. The groom is dressed in a dark suit, the bride radiant in what I imagine is traditional local wedding attire of white gown with distinctive blue braiding on the neck and front. I hope they forgive the two muddy lycra-wearing Australians who accidentally cycled into their picture

There's a gaggle of cyclists at the pizzeria on the Danube, but after our Ingolstadt indulgence we're both happy to keep cycling. Inspired by the illuminati, I start a long discourse on cycling and life.

'Cathie, cycling is the perfect metaphor for how a person lives their life. The journey is full of ups and downs but it's whether one can appreciate the easy downhills and learn to persevere on the tough uphills.'

'I feel like bratwurst and sauerkraut for lunch,' answers Cathie.

And so to Neustadt an der Donau, where there is only one cafe open. The sign on the door indicates a 1pm closing. It's 1.45pm. I tentatively open the door and am confronted by an imposing woman who looks like an amateur opera singer. Everything about her is large - big hair, billowing dress, loud voice, prominent make-up and most importantly, immense generosity as she indicates that she'll serve us before finally closing. The only item left on the menu is bratwurst! Alas for Cathie, it comes with chips. Not to be intimidated, Cathie smiles and says, 'Kraut?'

'Neine, pommes,' bellows the host.

We sit at a cosy table and look at the rain falling steadily outside. After fifty-two kilometres, our Gasthaus is somewhere in town.

The lady brings our plates, stacked high with chips and a bratwurst covered in mustard and tomato sauce. She wishes us 'bon appertit,' but returns a minute later with a steaming bowl of kraut. It warms our heart and our stomach. It's the sweetest best bowl of kraut I've ever eaten. The woman deserves to be on stage.

Once again, we are welcomed to our hotel earlier than the stated check-in time. Our room is clean and painted a pale orange. Alas, only one pillow each. No feathers. I decide to roll up my clean clothes and stuff them under the pillow. Lumpy, but effective.

For dinner, there is only one Gasthaus open. As we walk in, our two electric bike friends are walking out. We exchange greetings and I ask how their meal was. The both look pained. There is no other choice in town.

We sit in a booth and are served by a gaunt man with a beard and tired eyes. Schnitzel and chips, washed down with Bavarian beer. How bad can it be? The food is okay. However, it takes a very long time to arrive. There appears to be a disturbance in the kitchen. A woman with greasy hair and wearing tight jeans sways haphazardly towards our table. She leans close to me and says something slowly in German. Her breath smells of cigarettes and beer. I smile and try to explain I don't speak German. Her eyes cloud over. She looks back towards the kitchen and says something that sounds like a swear word. The owner rushes towards our table and with his hand on her shoulder gently leads the woman away. She shrugs free and lurches back towards us, repeating the word 'sorry' in English. The owner mutters under his breath and leads her away. At the end of the bar they have an intense conversation. He gestures to the exit. She sits defiantly at the bar. We ask for the bill.

Accommodation: Gasthof Gigl, Herzog-Ludwig Strasse 6, Neustadt an der Donau. Friendly hosts, good breakfast, wifi and storage for the bicycles. My score: 15/20

Restaurant: Not a lot to suggest in the evening. If possible, go to the Monarch Hotel in nearby Bad Goegging for dinner. It's decidedly upmarket, but better than what's on offer in town.

Distance cycled today: 52 km

What I should have said? 'Perhaps an Australian branch of the illuminati is in order?'

Chapter Ten

Neustadt to Regensburg, Germany

I'll avoid mentioning the breakfast this chapter. Oops, too late. Suffice to say, it was up to the usual high German standards. However, the weather is not playing its part in this fine journey. With only a week before the official start of summer, it's five degrees outside and the showers are becoming more frequent. Some people would call it *rain*, but I refuse to offer the weather gods any encouragement.

We attempt to break our record for speed at getting lost this morning. Not five hundred metres after leaving the hotel, I'm cursing quietly under my breath. Cathie is being far more intelligent, she's looking for signs pointing in the direction of Weltenburg. I've said my fifteenth rude word before she makes an executive decision and turns right along a dirt track. I follow, meekly. It's the correct way, of course.

Back on the levee and the dirt track is showing signs of puddle-weariness. We slow and warn each other of approaching wet patches. As a child, I'd delight in riding through puddles as fast as possible, hoping to splash water over my trailing companions. They'd swear and I'd glory in their expletives. I'd lift my feet off the pedals, lean back in the seat and whoop it up. I'm sorely tempted to enliven our Danube jaunt with a trip back to adolescence, but good manners and a healthy fear of my wife prevents me.

The showers get heavier.

'It's like having a wash with your clothes on,' I say.

Cathie does her best Marge Simpson impression and grunts

knowingly.

'If this keeps up, we won't have to wash our lycra tonight,' I add.

Luckily, our arrival at Weltenburg Abbey is just in time for Sunday Service. Situated on a peninsula in the river, the monastery was founded in the 7th century by monks and is believed to be the oldest monastery in Bavaria. The church, dedicated to Saint George was built in the early 18th century. In a sign of the times, the Abbey is now perhaps most famous for the oldest monastery brewery in the world, having been in operation since 1050. Their Dunkel beer has won the World Cup Award for dark lagers on three occasions.

Maybe that explains the full congregation this morning, but I imagine it's like that every Sunday in these surroundings. Who wouldn't want to spend time in this glorious Abbey. Cathie and I stand quietly at the rear while the Priest intones in Latin to his devout flock. Behind him is a glorious statue of Saint George on a horse, one hand wielding a sword at the dragon, in the other hand a lance with a flag fluttering at the tip. A fair maiden flinches, no doubt about to be eaten by the dragon until the intervention of the saintly horseman with the gold headwear.

I'm captivated by the sculptures of misshapen cherubs with what appear to be distended thighs and arms, holding up a railing framing the spectacular ceiling mural, itself a riot of colour and heavenly angels. I'm so focused on the cherubs that I hardly notice the Priest stop preaching and the congregation raise their tuneful voices in Sunday song. Cathie pokes me in the ribs and whispers that I should stop gazing skywards, lest somebody think I'm in prayer. I am. I'm praying for the cherubs and their distended limbs.

It's too early to sample the Dunkel beer. We have many kilometres to cycle before our attention can turn to the sainted brew.

But first a ferry cruise through the Weltenburg Narrows. This early in the morning, there are only ten passengers on board. All are cyclists. All wear long rain jackets and have waterproof panniers attached to their bicycles. Cathie and I feel woefully underdressed and unprepared for the weather.

Everyone stays inside the ferry cabin drinking coffee and eating pretzels, except us. We clamber onto the top deck and watch the Danube narrow, with high cliff walls on either side. The commentary, in German and English, is first-class. Did you know that the Danube is the only major European river that flows from west to east? Or that those three boulders over there, to our right, were three brothers who had a falling out and separated never to be reconciled. Or that imposing stone column is known as Napoleon's suitcase, because he was in such a hurry fleeing this region that he left his luggage behind. And that beautiful circular monument on the hill above Kelheim is a war memorial to all the soldiers killed in the Napoleonic Wars.

All this on a splendid twenty minute ferry cruise.

The captain performs a neat river-faring manoeuvre to dock. Five hundred metres from the wharf he turns the boat around 180 degrees until we're facing upstream again and puts it in neutral. The swift flowing Danube pulls us steadily downstream and close to the dock where the Captain simply powers up again and berths easily. I feel like applauding but eight other cyclists are waiting for Cathie and I to remove our bikes from the lower deck so they can be on their way. We hurriedly clatter up the gang plank and are immediately overtaken by all eight hardy souls.

We shrug and follow behind. I noticed while disembarking that they all have maps in waterproof holders attached to their handlebars. Although recent history proves a map is no guarantee of being on the correct path, we hastily pick up the pace to keep the Eight Horseman of the Danube in sight. They cycle stoically into the showers and wind, consulting their maps at each juncture, debating in German the correct route. Cathie and I swig on our water bottle and wait.

Left, it is.

The Danube is flowing faster and wider now. It's here that the cruise ships can navigate the river with ease. Upstream of Kelheim, they must use the canal to avoid the Narrows and the many sandbars of the upper river.

The Danube runs through a natural valley, with the ground rising on either side of the river before giving way to dark forest. Occasionally, I catch a glimpse of a hawk hovering above.

The German Conference of Lost Cyclists is on again. Four female cyclists want to go left. Two men agree. The other two men, louder and more assertive, strongly advise right. The sign points left. Cathie looks at me before mounting Jenny and taking the left option. I agree. Having always favoured the left side of politics, I figure we might as well always go left whenever in doubt. The eight follow our new leader, my wife!

And true to form, Cathie leads us safely into Bad Abbach, a quiet town with a cobblestone main street. There appears to be only one cafe open and while the other eight keep riding, Cathie and I hesitantly park our bikes under an awning opposite and prepare to go inside. Removing my helmet, I notice a lot of people eating hearty German food through the window of the Gasthaus opposite. I'd choose a Gasthaus over a cafe every time.

We enter meekly, dripping water on the wooden floor before being greeted by a middle-aged woman in traditional costume who ushers us to the only available table. We hang our sodden jackets on the coat hook and try not to look too embarrassed at leaving a trail of water from entrance to table. I order a local speciality, a delicious broth with an oversized liver dumpling stranded in the middle. Cathie opts for the asparagus-cream soup. Both cost only three Euros. We slurp contentedly and are quickly full. Our empty bowls are immediately removed and replaced by our second course, a large plate of roast pork with zeppelin-shaped dumplings. It is salty, rich and hugely satisfying. I feel like ordering a jug of beer and dancing on the table, but instead lean back in my sturdy chair and contemplate how my stomach seems to have swollen. One could say it's distended, much like the friendly cherubs back at the Abbey.

We reluctantly leave and walk out into the rain. As if on cue, our friends with the e-bikes cycle past and gesture for us to join them. We cycle the afternoon together, exchanging pleasantries through mime and the occasional shared word, such as 'rain' 'cold' 'wet' 'scheisse!'

The rain increases on the outskirts of Regensburg. The football games being played on water-logged fields beside the river cheer me. All the players are middle-aged men, overweight and slow, although they play with the vigour and dedication of men half their age. The cycle path is now an obstacle course of puddles and wheel ruts. We all cycle slowly, picking our line through the watery maze. I sneeze and nearly swerve into the river.

The friendly couple, Eric and Frida escort us to the main square of town before leaving. They still have another ten kilometres to cycle to their pre-booked accommodation. I call 'tomorrow' as they cycle away, sure we will see them again.

I booked the accommodation for tonight but have jotted down only scant directions. We stop and ask the way to the Regensburg B&B from a very handsome couple who speak excellent English. At first, they look confused. The man, who wears a long woollen overcoat says, 'Regensburg Hotel?'

'Bed and Breakfast,' I reply.

He looks down at my address again.

'It is three kilometres that way.' He points down a wide street.

I understand it's too far away for him to offer a detailed

description, so we thank them and slowly ride away into the increasing downpour. After five minutes of riding along the wide thoroughfare beside cars with their headlights blazing in the early afternoon, I stop to ask directions from a young man with two children, each riding a bike.

'The hotel?' he asks.

'B&B,' I repeat. What is it about their insistence on calling our quaint accommodation a hotel?

He smiles and readily offers precise directions.

Five minutes later we arrive at the Regensburg B&B. It's a five-storey strip hotel on a busy main road. It seems as if 'B&B' is the name of a German hotel chain. I hadn't read the description very well.

Cold and very wet, we walk to the front door. It's locked. A sign informs us, in multiple languages that it opens in two hours. Another sign tells us to enter our booking code in the door lock and we'll be granted entry. I shuffle around in my panniers and find the code. It doesn't work. I enter the numbers again. The door remains locked.

Another sign details how we can pay with a credit card at the machine below and we'll be granted entry. Despite having already booked, I figure we have nothing to lose. My credit card works and we wheel the bikes into a tiled entry foyer. I cannot find anywhere to leave Jenny and Craig so we park and lock them beside the vending machine. While I'm doing this, Cathie puts three Euro in the machine and receives two cups of pre-fab coffee. We don't care. It's hot and strong. Our room is on the third floor and resembles a sealed capsule. We turn the air-conditioning up high and strip out of our saturated clothing.

Two hours later, I go down to reception and am greeted by a rather angry young woman who informs me the bicycle garage is downstairs in the car park and would I kindly remove the muddy and dripping bikes from the foyer. I explain about the confusion in entry procedures and she mellows somewhat. Although she does appear to take some glee in telling me the nearest restaurant is fifteen minutes walk away. It's pouring rain outside.

I have perhaps booked the most inappropriate motel possible.

Fearing the worst, I suggest to Cathie we catch a taxi into town and eat our fill at the best Gasthaus we can find. As my loving wife does with all offers of food, she accepts willingly.

The Ratskeller restaurant is warm and inviting and a pretty red-haired waitress leads us to a table and offers to translate the menu. It's not necessary. We both want beef sauerbraten with red cabbage and dumplings. And two jugs of beer. The restaurant is one of the oldest in Regensburg, located as the name suggests in the cellar of the town hall and suitably crowded with couples and noisy groups knocking back beers and schnitzels. The arched roof is decorated with colourful paintings of Knights helmets. We quickly forget a day spent in the rain and contemplate what to eat for dessert. Apple strudel looms large on the menu and on the plate the waitress places before me. I'm pleased we ordered one to share.

In the late evening we wander the narrow lanes and cobblestone streets of the old town. The cathedral is suitably Gothic and bleak, rearing up from the town square like a haunted castle. Regensburg has a bloodstained history. In 1096, on the way to the First Crusade, the well-named Peter the Hermit lead a mob who tried to convert the town Jews. When the citizens resisted, they were killed. In 1809 the town was ransacked during the Battle of Ratisbon and at the end of the Second World War was home to one of the largest Displaced Person Camps in Germany. Such a beautiful town. So much bloodshed.

All is much quieter now. The restaurants and cafes are well-frequented by wealthy and handsome locals. The rain has ceased and I can't resist taking numerous photos of the traditional costumes in the window displays. I'm particularly impressed with the gold braid lining of the beige-coloured men's shorts. The women's outfits are delightful bodice revealing designs of white ruffled tops and brightly-coloured skirts.

'What say we come here first thing tomorrow and buy you that fetching green ensemble,' I suggest.

'Are they waterproof?' Cathie deadpans.

Accommodation: Regensburg Hotel B&B, Landshuter Strasse 111-113A Regensburg. A strip hotel with parking, wifi and cheap rooms. Breakfast is a little impersonal and costs extra. My score: 13/20

Restaurant: Ratskeller Restaurant, Rathausplatz 1, Regensburg. Friendly waiters, hearty traditional menu, lovely atmosphere, highly recommended. My score: 17/20

Distance cycled today: 60 km

Actual distance: 45 km

What I should have said? 'Another apple strudel, perhaps?'

Chapter Eleven

Regensburg to Deggendorf, Germany

In our vacuum-sealed highway hotel, we feel like shrivelled waifs waiting for the morning and perhaps news of a change in the weather. I look out the window. The rain has increased. Reluctantly we shrug into dry, but still dirty lycra before heading down to the breakfast room where we are fed the type of soulless meal you'd expect in such a hotel. We sigh and look out at the cars sloshing past on the main road.

We retrieve our bikes, crusty with hard-dried mud from the dark car park and pedal through the rush hour of Regensburg. The rain relents and some of the caked mud falls off Craig and Jenny, although their gear changes this morning feel less than precise. We cycle slowly through the morning streets of the old town where the Cathedral is imposing and bleak against the grey sky.

We cross the stone bridge under repair, the workers erecting scaffolding on the far side as we cycle nervously over a temporary walkway before cruising along a dirt track of the riverside park. A man calls his two dalmatians to heel as soon as they set eyes on us. Cathie slows warily and I attempt my usual, 'G'day fella' spiel, putting the dogs at ease if only they understood English. They run skittishly alongside me. The man calls again in a dog-friendly language and they leave us alone and go off chasing each other. A minute later we reach a dead-end with the Danube on one side and a creek on the other. There is nowhere to go but back from where we came and over the same ancient bridge.

Lost and only ninety-four kilometres to go.

We eventually find the correct path alongside suburban houses and over a more recent and much more imposing bridge with semi-trailers and buses sloshing through the morning. Out of town, the Danube widens and we look north towards small villages at the foot of misty hills. They appear cold and quiet as if still bunkered down for winter, even though it's - quick check of calendar - precisely four days until the start of summer.

We slug through a dreary thirty kilometres before out first stop at Worth an der Donau, predictably enough at a backerei where the woman with blond hair piled high on her head and held there with a bone-coloured clasp, looks taken aback at the amount of water dripping from our clothes onto her clean shop floor. I offer a meek apology and make matters worse by leaving my backpack on a chair. One stern glance from the owner and I quickly remove it, placing it out of sight under the table. It's soon joined by my helmet, sodden gloves, earmuffs and bandana. We hang our jackets from the hooks on the wall near the bathroom. They drip, like water torture as we eat two hazelnut danish and drink coffee. Our presence is soon forgotten by the woman as another cyclist comes in and places his helmet, backpack and gloves on the table. The nerve of some people! Fortunately he understands German and is quickly told to remove them.

As we wait for the rain to stop and debate whether that will occur anytime this year, I spy an outdoor clothing store opposite the cake shop. Why not, I think? Cathie waits patiently in the warmth while I venture across the road and look at the racks of waterproof jackets on display at the entrance. A bright orange jacket looks appealing at only fifty Euros and the red goretex jacket at two-hundred and sixty Euros would definitely be waterproof.

The owner comes out and greets me by saying in English, 'You want waterproof?' I look at the dripping sky in answer. He elaborately lays an exceedingly ugly royal blue jacket with light blue and white horizontal stripes on the table.

'This is waterproof,' he says.

'And very ugly,' I reply, not really expecting him to understand.

He laughs, 'You want pretty or you want dry?'

'Uumm, both,' I suggest.

'Come with me,' he beckons. I follow him into the shop, row after row of merino wool vests, goretex jackets, ski gloves, waterproof pants and those really ugly knotty socks that hikers wear and claim they never need washing. Yeah right.

The owner stands beside a long rack of fire-engine red goretex jackets and runs his hand along the sleeve of one.

'You want this. Three hundred Euros. Keep you dry in a monsoon.'

He sees me wince at the price.

'Where you from?' he asks.

'Australia,' I answer.

'I just shipped football boots to Sydney. Only cost seventeen Euro to send them. I can do the same with your jacket.'

'I need it now not in Sydney,' I say, perhaps unnecessarily.

'Then three hundred Euros or the ugly one,' he says.

'How much is ugliness this year?' I ask, expecting to be stung for one hundred Euro.

'Twenty Euros,' he says.

'Twenty?' I repeat.

'Ugly is cheap,' he says, before adding, 'It's old stock.'

Yeah, 1970 I imagine, but there's no doubting it is goretex and it looks like it fits. So I offer to try it on to humour my new friend.

Yes, fits perfectly.

The owner grins, but doesn't say a word.

In one last attempt to gain some credibility, I reach for the orange jacket on sale for fifty Euro and say, 'This one's better, isn't it?'

He shakes his head and takes it from the coat hanger, turning it inside out to show me the stitching.

'Only one stitch here, on the shoulder,' he says, before adding, 'It's Italian.'

I suspect he's means *Piaggo* Italian not *Ferrari* Italian.

I give in. Anybody who tries to sell a twenty Euro jacket before a fifty Euro one can be trusted. I look in the mirror and decide ugliness suits me. He helpfully cuts the tag from the zip. The jacket is mine.

'I will return if it's not waterproof,' I say.

'Goodbye, my friend,' he responds.

I walk triumphantly across the road and enter the backerei wearing my new striped goretex waterproof jacket.

'You look like a Peter Steyvesant cigarette commercial from the 1970s,' Cathie says.

'Thank you,' I reply.

'It wasn't a compliment,' she adds.

'It's goretex!'

'I didn't know it'd been invented that long ago,' she says.

I show her the double stitching, the sleeves that clasp tightly around my wrist to repel the wind, the fetching cream coloured flap across the neck under the zip and lastly, I flip the hood over my head and pull the tags tight.

'100% waterproof,' I say.

Cathie grins. I know how stupid I look, but frankly I don't care because the rain continues to pour down outside and I have a waterproof jacket and Cathie can now wear my white cycling jacket over her polartec for added protection. We will both be warm and dry. At last.

We walk out of the backerei like two Michelin roly-poly figures about to go cycling. The track follows the river and we cycle through steady showers, both smiling.

Beads of water gather at my sleeve but my arms stay dry. I feel impregnable.

Our mood lifts. We cycle past a football field and I stop to take a photo of the club insignia painted on the clubhouse. Our son is a football journalist in Australia and I can't resist sending him photos of obscure German team crests.

At lunchtime we divert to Straubing and admire the Gothic town hall, painted orange with a fetching balcony overlooking the town square. In the pouring rain, the square is empty. The owner of a shoe store stands at the entrance under an awning, waiting for customers. He takes a final drag of a cigarette and blows smoke into the cold air.

We nervously enter the Rohrl Gasthaus in the main square. In the lobby is a reception desk and a stand laden with jackets. The woman at the counter indicates we should leave our jackets here and enter the restaurant through the ornate doors to our left.

'But what if someone steals my jacket?' I whisper to Cathie.

She hangs her two jackets next to a full-length black leather coat.

'You really think they'd take yours instead of all the expensive jackets hanging here,' she says.

I have become very attached to my ugly outerwear. I shrug and hang it on the only remaining hook.

'I'll never find another one like it,' I say.

'That's for sure,' Cathie answers, her voice heavy with sarcasm.

Lunch is superb. We start with a spicy goulash soup accompanied by warm bread rolls. I can't resist asking for another roll. I dip and slurp and scoop and generally show all the other diners how uncouth one hungry Australian can be. The first course is so filling, we share roast veal and dumplings for the main course. It's rich and hearty and I almost consider suggesting we stay here for the rest of the afternoon and night, eating and drinking. I consult the map on our iPad. Forty kilometres to Deggendorf.

'We could,' I begin.

'Let's keep going,' Cathie interrupts, reading my mind. She smiles, 'We'll see just how waterproof your jacket is.'

The afternoon unwinds in a haze of rain and sodden wheat fields and the fast-rising Danube. Outside Bogen, a white church stands high on a hill, it's tower regal against the gloomy skies. We keep our heads down and cycle in a slow but steady rhythm.

Beside the river, with few people around and little barge traffic everything seems muted. A white crane stands on a wooden pier, a lone speedboat moored near the bank bobs jauntily and on the verandah of a wooden single-storey house a dog sleep on a rug. There are few villages. The fields open out and a hawk flies from the forest and pirouettes above a ploughed paddock, on the watch for scurrying mice.

In the late afternoon, we arrive at the pretty town of Deggendorf, scene of yet another pogrom against the Jews, this time in the 14th century.

The cobblestone square is a riot of brightly coloured buildings and masses of flowers planted in large pots under ornate lamp-posts. The square is bookended by a lovely old town hall with a Gothic tower and the 14th century Church of Saints Peter and Paul. And in between these two icons is our hotel. For once I appear to have booked the best hotel in town.

The friendly receptionist even encourages us to wheel our dripping bicycles through the main foyer and out the back door where they are securely locked in a warm garage. There are lots of bikes in the garage. Our room is on the top floor at the rear. We're both cold and weary. As soon as I enter, I strip out of my sodden clothes and jump in the shower. There is no hot water.

I phone reception. She explains that lots of cyclists have arrived this afternoon and they've all obviously indulged in very long hot showers. She suggests a free upgrade to a front room. I don't quite understand how that room will have more hot water but readily agree. The front room is large and warm and offers a lovely view of the town square. And, yes, it has hot water.

I contemplate singing in the shower but my beautiful wife has already been through enough difficulties today.

For dinner we go no further than downstairs to the restaurant where I order a splendidly large and rich roast duck with potato dumplings and red cabbage. Cathie chooses the roast pork.

'We cycled ninety-five kilometres today,' I say, raising my beer for a toast.

'And only ninety were in the rain,' Cathie smiles.

'Have you seen tomorrow's forecast,' I say.

'Sunny,' she nods.

We can't quite believe it, but we eat and drink to celebrate the expected arrival of summer.

Accommodation: Hotel Gasthof Hottl, Luitpoldplatz 22, Deggendorf. Friendly staff, wifi, storage for bicycles, excellent breakfast and ideal location in the centre of town. My score: 16/20

Restaurant: Hotel Gasthoff Hottl Restaurant. Hearty meals in pleasant surroundings. My score: 16/20

Distance cycled today: 95 km

Actual distance: 82 km

What I should have said? 'Blue and white horizontal stripes are very fashionable in some parts of the world, I'll have you know.'

Chapter Twelve

Deggendorf to Passau, Germany

I look out our hotel window this morning and see a strange bright orb in the sky. In the town square below my window stand four businessmen, jackets slung casually over their shoulders. They are wearing sunglasses. True to the forecast, summer has arrived.

Cathie and I eat breakfast surrounded by brass candleabras and ornate light fittings in a lovely dining room. Today's addition to the extensive menu is bacon and scrambled eggs, tropical fruit and doughnuts. Rotund men in crisply ironed shirts and polyester trousers hover around the doughnut plate, like jilted lovers waiting to be forgiven. A man slips a second pastry into a brown paper bag on his way out.

The receptionist asks me if I had a hot shower this morning.

'Yep, used every last drop of water,' I joke.

Before leaving Deggendorf, Cathie and I wander the streets. In the square, market stallholders arrange their wares, van drivers wheel crates of vegetables into supermarkets and an old man sits outside a cafe, his eyes closed enjoying the warmth of the morning.

My phone rings. I anxiously walk to a quiet corner of the square to answer it. It's our youngest son, Joe excitedly telling us that he has just had his first major piece published on the Guardian Australia website. We're enormously proud. Cathie whispers to me, 'Another writer in the family.' We send him kisses and rush to the nearest wifi cafe to seek out Joe's piece. We both read it, torn between pride and missing him terribly.

The sun is shining and it's time to be cycling along the Danube, once again. The river is fast-flowing, a water police boat struggles to make it upstream, the low bank is threatened by waves slapping against the shore. We ride on the extreme left of the path, just in case.

Neidholden is a small village boasting an ancient monastery, a church with twin spires and an aeronautical museum. We lean our bikes against the church wall and I tentatively turn the handle of the huge wooden door of the church. It creaks and we quietly enter. No-one is around. We whisper in reverence at the beautiful white and gold colour scheme. Behind the altar is an extravagant pink marble and gold sculpture of angels and shepherds. On either side of the church, where the stations of the Cross normally are, is a glass-encased figure reclining. I assume this means there is an important person interned underneath. I've seen this in many churches of course, but the unusual aspect here is the humourous poses of each reclining figure. One holds a clasp of sticks; another appears to be asleep with a book resting on his chest; another casually rests his head on one arm, as if he's about to reach for the remote control to switch channels; yet another is a skeleton. There is a rope preventing us from getting too close to properly investigate.

The monastery was founded as far back as the 8th century on this site, although the church dates from the late 13th century. The interior was redesigned in Baroque style in 1720 by the architect Johann Michael Fischer. It's an impressive spectacle with unobstrusive stucco pillars, white painted columns and archways and numerous elaborate frescos. We are indeed privileged to have such intimate access.

In the next village of Winzer, we stop at a backerei. Apple danish for me, a sensational Sicilian lemon cake for Cathie. We have been to Sicily, but have never had a cake quite as delicious as this one. The sun streams through the cafe window as we debate whether we should order another cake. We make do by gazing at the dizzying array of pastries on offer. The owner proudly stands behind her counter, serving an endless stream of adoring customers.

Surprisingly, it's much quieter on the path today. I expected everyone to be outdoors taking in the glorious sunshine. I whoop down an embankment from the Danube and run straight into a swarm of bugs, swallowing dozens and coughing up only a few. I take a long swig of water and remember not to open my mouth any more on this trip unless it's to answer Cathie or to eat.

On a boulder beside the river, I spy a shiny steel object that reminds me of a coffee tamper. I stop to investigate. It's a scale model of the planet Jupiter. One hundred metres further along is another coffee tamper, slightly bigger, which is Orion. Next is the distinctive ringed Saturn, then a coffee tamper for leprechaun baristas, titled Mercury. I look far ahead and see a replica of the sun, large and yellow and dwarfing everything else. We are on the PlanetariumWeg, just before the town of Vilshofen.

Let it be known that Vilshofen is hereby awarded the 'best bicycle arrival in a Danube town' award. As well as the educational cruise through the solar system, we're treated to a lovely bridge crossing. We stop half-way across and watch as a light plane takes off only a few hundred metres away at the airport on the banks of the Danube. The pilot deftly banks across the Danube at a height of no more than fifty metres. I'm tempted to wave but he looks busy at the controls.

We cycle across the bridge and ride the cobblestone main street. Like every Bavarian village, the buildings are beautifully restored, painted yellow, red, pink or green with white trim and often decorated with a mural or delicate flourishes like fine embroidery. Cathie remarks that they are so well restored it's impossible to tell whether they are one hundred or five hundred years old. We sit at an outdoor table in the sun and enjoy a strudel and coffee. Yes, that's our second cake for the morning. It's very pleasant to be wearing only shorts and a short-sleeved jersey for a change.

We cycle on the right bank of the Danube. The hills rise sharply on either side of the river and are covered in dense forest. Occasionally there's a break in the trees for a farm with meadows of cows. After one long downhill with mouth firmly closed in case of bugs, a sign directs us to the small village of Sandbach, through a tunnel under the train line and to the bank of the Danube.

But there is no path to ride alongside the river?

On the opposite bank, one hundred and fifty metres away is a punt, beginning its journey across to pick up two grateful Australians. I'm thrilled beyond words. A cruise on the Danube! For 1.50 Euro! I can barely contain my excitement. I take out my camera and film the slowly approaching punt. Cathie smiles contentedly. She knows I'm a child at heart.

The punt docks with a screeching of metal on bitumen and the stout woman captain holds up her hand, instructing the childish cyclist to wait until the gate has been opened before boarding. We are the only passengers. In excellent English, the captain says she'll be back in five minutes. She rides her bicycle off the boat and disappears through the tunnel.

'A toilet break,' explains Cathie.

I walk along the deck of the punt, rubbing my hands over the huge wheel, taking photo after photo of Craig and Jenny facing each other, their tyres touching like the young lovers they are. The river is a romantic backdrop. Craig doesn't talk to me as much as he used to, now Jenny is here. I miss our long chats where I did most of the talking and he offered a pithy creak or bump to interrupt my reverie.

The Captain returns and immediately casts off. We putter across the river, our rear section being dragged downstream by the current. The Captain tells us of three cyclists who were on board yesterday.

'They were young men, cycling to Turkey. Two thousand five hundred kilometres, but only in twenty-five days,' she shakes her head, 'One hundred kilometres a day. How do they see anything?'

I can only agree. I'd love to cycle to Turkey, but I'd need two months or more.

'Yesterday rain,' the Captain says. She looks at the blue sky, only a few wispy clouds on the horizon.

'Tomorrow rain. And the next day more rain,' she adds.

'Today beautiful,' I answer. I don't want to think of tomorrow, not when I'm on a Danube cruise! We dock and wave goodbye to the Captain. Five cyclists are already waiting to board. A few kilometres along we stop for lunch at a riverside restaurant. We sit at an outdoor table and watch the long narrow cruise boats steam past.

I think of the television commercials I've seen back in Australia advertising cruises down the Danube. They are always packaged as the pinnacle of luxury with images of a well-dressed couple sipping champagne, smiling and pointing to a castle on a bend in the river. The buzz phrases are five-star dining, royal banquets and panoramic vistas.

The gruff waiter brings us each a steaming bowl of fish soup and a crusty chunk of bread. It's dark and rich and delicious and I decide it's a 'bicyclist's banquet' at the princely sum of three Euro. I order another beer.

A group of cycling families pull up at the restaurant. The two men ride sporty hybrid bikes, each with rear panniers. The three daughters ride girl's bikes, the youngest has streamers flowing from her handlebars. The only mother has a bike trailer with a child aboard, surrounded by nappies and other clothes. She picks the child out of the trailer and lets him run around on the grass beside the river. The men have already ordered beers. The daughters sit on the grass and look after the child while Mum searches in the trailer for a fresh nappy.

We cycle easily through the afternoon along the river path, overtaking an increasing number of cruise ships. I could cycle all day in this perfect sunshine.

Passau is an extraordinarily beautiful town located at the confluence of three rivers and home to a university and a burgeoning tourist industry based on cruise boats. The town shines with youthful vitality and optimism. On this glorious afternoon, young people are strolling through the green parks, drinking beer at bars alongside the river or just hanging out on the cobblestone streets.

Our hotel is above a chicken shop and ominously comes with two sets of earplugs. When I enquire about this, the young woman says there's a disco every second Wednesday in the pub opposite. Today is Tuesday. Our room is spartan and compact but ideally located near the city centre.

We quickly change into street clothes and wander across town to the Inn River. We sit on a bench seat beside a lovely flower bed and look at the reflections in the river of a church across the water. I don't want to move, so serene is the scene. Every few seconds a young person cycles past. Three girls, with tumbling hair and tight jeans relax on the grass and make eye-contact with the two bearded hipsters drinking beer at the bar.

Eventually, we stroll along the banks of the Inn towards the point where it meets the wide Danube. A child, watched by his young father rides a tri-cycle in the park; two office workers loosen their ties and share a pizza on the grass; a jogger in singlet and lurid green shorts stretches against a bollard at the pier and my wife and I gawk open-mouthed at one of the loveliest towns we've had the pleasure to visit.

St Stephens Cathedral is a stunning example of Italian Baroque built by the architect Carlo Lurago, also responsible for the charming pilgrimage church at Maria Taferl, further down the Danube. Home to the largest Cathedral organ in the world with over seventeen thousand pipes, St Stephens is a magnet for cruise ship passengers. Consequently, our visit is accompanied by the whirring of numerous video cameras and the snap of a thousand shutters. It's a beautiful place of worship, with or without all we tourists.

We walk to the Danube shore where I'm thrilled to discover the bronze bust of Bavarian poet, Emerenz Meier on the pier. Nearby is a plaque quoting one of her poems which playfully pokes fun at all the male poets who spend their days writing poetry and 'observing' the world, while their wife 'salts the dumplings,' 'kills the bugs,' 'washes the dishes,' and 'cleans the rooms.' Cathie spends an inordinate amount of time reading the poem. She looks at me, knowingly.

'What?' I ask.

We eat dinner in a cute garden shed of the Pensione Goldenes Schiff. The lovely waitress, a woman who we first see this evening carrying a keg of beer into the bar, helps us with the menu. She suggests vegetable dumplings for Cathie while I choose the goulash. Both meals come with a fresh salad that could adequately feed the entire University of Passau football team. We order two pilseners and contemplate the warmth of a summer evening settling over the garden.

After eating more than our fill, we wander along the dock where the numerous cruise boats are moored. On deck are rich couples dressed in elegant pastel colours, drinking cocktails and watching the fast-flowing Danube. In the park at the end of town, shaggy-haired students juggle a football, four young men with dyed hair drink beer and a girl with blonde hair bites her fingernails and reads a text book.

We sit on the same bench seat as we did earlier this afternoon and watch the glorious reflection on the Inn River slowly recede into the night.

Accommodation: StadtHotel Passau, Grosse Klingergasse 17, Passau. A curious hotel above a fast food restaurant. Good location, rooms small and comfortable, could be noisy when the nearby disco is on, no wifi. My score: 13/20

Restaurant: Goldenes Schiff Pensione, Unterer Sand 8, Passau. Lovely staff, big servings, pleasant atmosphere. My score: 16/20.

Distance cycled: 58 km

Actual distance: 56 km

What I should have said? 'How many cruise ship passengers can you fit into a church?'

Chapter Thirteen

Passau, Germany to Wesenufer, Austria

At the risk of sounding repetitive, I look out the window this morning and curse the rain. We stoically shrug into our winter wet weather gear, glance at the calendar on my iPad and slowly cycle around the corner to a backerei for our fruhstuck. The considerate chef has handpainted the hard-boiled eggs in multiple colours to cheer us. It does. We eat it all and pay the ridiculously cheap price of E3.99, before cycling over the bridge on the Inn River. I glance back at Passau. A beautiful town, even in the rain.

For two kilometres, we cycle on a narrow path through the suburb of Innstadt looking at the backyards of numerous houses. It seems as if every second house has a vegetable garden and ramshackle glasshouse for growing seedlings. Stacks of rough cut logs line the fences ready for next winter. Or perhaps tomorrow?

A man in grey overalls works on his lawn-mower in a shed. A dog barks at a crow in the tree. A mother sits on a chair on the back deck and slowly rocks her pram.

I love these paths. They remind me of riding trains when I was a child and peering into the backyards of suburbs as we raced past. I was always thrilled to see what people made of their own little garden space. I love coming across eccentric gardens with gnomes hiding under oak trees or standing guard at the ramshackle shed. Or discovering a full-size football goal with net attached or rows of grapevines and fruit trees or hand built fish ponds. The good folk of Innstadt prove that the world of suburbia doesn't have to be bland and conformist.

Within a few kilometres we come upon a sign welcoming us to Austria. I always feel immense satisfaction cycling across a border.

Perhaps I'm kidding myself I've cycled a great distance, but it's thrilling to enter a new territory and 'spot the differences.'

Uumm ... it looks just like Germany only the rain is falling harder. I'm not blaming Austria for that.

Actually, the forest beside the Danube does rise more steeply and it certainly looks darker and more gloomy. The Austrian meadows appear to be carved out of the mountain side, so steep and inaccessible and yet it's apparent someone up there is farming, even if the ground is snow-covered for six months of the year.

After the village of Kasten, the valley narrows considerably and there seems hardly enough space for a road and bike path before the forest and hills take over. Wispy clouds, lower than the hills float down the Danube like ethereal barges. We giggle like school children at the sight of our first Austrian castle on a hill. The rain falls heavier and we decide to stop for cake and coffee at Engelhartzell. It's an old cafe, blue stucco on the outside with big windows and white-painted window boxes. Inside it has wooden bench tables and chairs with floral napkins and placemats. I eat a light sweet cheesecake and Cathie makes do with an espresso and apple juice. I enquire if she's not feeling well?

'Why, because I didn't order a cake?'

'No ... well, yes,' I say.

She smiles and reaches across to grab my fork and take a large bite of my cheesecake.

'I knew you'd be happy to share,' she says.

The rain falls heavier as soon as we jump back on the bikes and pedal along the road for a kilometre. It's torrential. We look across the river to see three hardy cyclists pedalling through the tumult. We're on the wrong side of the river. We quickly backtrack to town and search for the cross river ferry. In the rain, we'd missed the sign.

It's without doubt the cutest Danube ferry imaginable, painted dark shades of green, brown and red and constructed of timber. The Captain sits in a little booth like a man selling pies at a kiosk. He smiles as we squelch onboard and takes our money ruefully. Perhaps he thinks the Austrian Tourist Board should pay our fares to compensate for the weather.

I love the ferry ride as we get to stand under an awning, out of the downpour for the three minute journey. I'm considering suggesting a deal to the Captain. Can we stay on board until the rain stops, crossing and re-crossing the glorious Danube, watching the swallows play above the surface, the cruise boats arrowing past, the barges puttering upstream. Just to stand here and not think about the rain.

Then it's back to the sloshing.

It's a beautiful section of the river with mist curling above the forest, the river wide and fast-flowing, the occasional glimpse of a stately house set amongst the trees. We slow to a gentle pace and take it all in. A barge labours upstream, the Captain in his warm wheelhouse waves to us. We pass a small white church with a red tile roof and three circular windows like portholes, appropriately facing the river. A two-level cruise ship floats along. There appears to be only a scattering of passengers, sitting in the glass-enclosed top deck playing cards.

Before we know it, we've arrived in Wesenufer a small village on the right side of the Danube which is our destination for the evening. It's lunchtime. We ride through deserted streets with a smattering of houses and slowly climb a very steep hill to where our guesthouse is located. I tentatively knock at the door. An old man wearing slippers and corduroy trousers answers the door, quizzically.

'I'm sorry, we're early,' I say, perhaps stating the obvious. 'Could we leave our bicycles here while we walk into town to have lunch?'

'You can check in,' he says. He directs us to the garage where we park our bicycles and then leads us to our room. It has a lovely view down the slope to the Danube and across the river to the forest rising on the far bank.

We gratefully remove our drenched clothing and have a warm shower. We drape our freshly-washed lycra over the heaters before walking back into town. The rain has stopped. It's a very quiet village with few people outdoors. At the hotel, we walk into the restaurant to see the owner on his hands and knees scrubbing the floor. It's immediately apparent the restaurant is closed.

Open for the season ... from tomorrow.

We cross the road to a grocery store. The sign on the wall informs us it's closed.

My stomach rumbles.

Next door to the grocery store is a newly-restored building with tables and chairs outside and a large glassed-in entrance way. It looks like a museum. We nervously open the door and step inside. There is no-one around. On a long table covered in a yellow tablecloth are numerous empty wine glasses and dirty plates. We walk down a corridor and enter a lovely restaurant with a white-washed arched ceiling, narrow windows opening out to the river and tables set ready for dining. It's empty. On one table rests a menu. I sneak a glance. My stomach rumbles even louder.

We hear voices coming from the other end of the long corridor.

'Perhaps there's a bar with snacks,' I say hopefully.

We investigate. It is indeed a splendid long bar with a woman wearing black trousers and a white blouse. Her hair is flame red and tied in a ponytail. She speaks perfect English.

Despite the lack of customers, the restaurant is open. The waitress leads us back to the dining area and allows us to choose whichever table we wish. We order two beers and she tells us a staff member will take our order soon.

I turn the menu over and read that this is 'a workshop hotel designed for people with psychological disabilities to enable an active integration into the working world.' It can accommodate thirty people and teach them all the necessary skills required to gain work in the service industries.

A woman with minimal English takes our order. She is also wearing the black and white garments of service staff. She smiles at my pitiful attempts to pronounce the German menu. Cathie and I both have a simple but tasty beef broth soup followed by a sensational grilled chicken and risotto with asparagus. Before I've finished the main course, Cathie asks the waitress what I'm already thinking.

'Are you open tonight?'

They are. We order another beer and contemplate our good fortune.

We finally drag ourselves away from the restaurant to spend the afternoon in our large bedroom, watching the boats cruise slowly past on the Danube. Cathie sleeps. I take notes of our journey so far and check the forecast for the next few days. Rain, with potential flooding on the Danube. The window fogs with warmth from the heater.

While Cathie sleeps, I retire to the breakfast room where I sip a coke and watch the cruise boats stuttering by. On a bend in the river downstream is a castle. I wonder who lives there? Old or new money? An aristocrat down on his luck with only a pitiful inheritance and a cold castle to call home. Perhaps his wife has left him and his son visits for a few weeks in summer? Or an executive at BMW, who spends his week in Munich and weekends at the castle, working on flow charts and sales figures, design plans and exhibition brochures, rarely noticing the sublime views?

The afternoon drifts. I'm happy to be warm and dry.

For dinner we walk back to the Seminaakultur an der Donau.

Tonight I order pork with rosti and salad followed by apricot pancakes and beer from a barrel. We are content.

Accommodation: Privatzimmer Feiken, Wesenufer 65, Wesennufer, Austria. Friendly warm guesthouse with a variety of rooms on offer. Wifi and bike storage. Some rooms have sensational views. My score: 15/20

Restaurant: Seminarkultur an der Donau, Wesenufer, Austria. Lovely atmosphere, excellent staff and service, good quality food at a reasonable price. The Seminarkultur now also has rooms available upstairs. My score: 16/20.

Distance cycled: 37 km

Actual distance: 37 km

What I should have said? 'I don't suppose you need a deckhand for the afternoon, Captain?'

Chapter Fourteen

Wesenufer to Linz, Austria

The morning dawns bleak and cloudy with the certainty of rain. We cruise down the hill from our B&B and cycle back towards Passau. No, we're not giving up but the bike path is on the left side of the Danube and the closest bridge is two kilometres upstream. We cycle through sleepy Wesenufer and the only people out this early, apart from us are two men in military-style uniforms. They are marching purposely down the main street as if on important State business. In Wesenufer?

Finally heading in the correct direction, I cast a hopeful glance at the sky. A bank of dark clouds are closing in behind us while downstream I can see blue sky. Perhaps I'm hallucinating. I check which way the wind is blowing. As I imagined, it's pushing the rain clouds toward us.

'If we speed up perhaps we can outrun them,' I suggest.

'You want to race the weather?' Cathie asks, looking dubiously behind her.

'Only until Linz,' I say.

'That's sixty kilometres,' she says. 'You propose we sprint for three hours.'

We laugh at the absurdity of it and decide to ignore the clouds. We're on a lovely small road close to the river with only one car having passed us in the first eight kilometres. On the other side of the road is a steep-sided hill covered in forest, occasionally opening out to a farm usually with a sturdy white-painted house facing the river, a wooden barn at right angles to the house and a neat front garden. Always a neat garden.

A large sign written in German interrupts our cycle. From what I can tell, in one kilometre we have a choice of three ferries. Two will take us across to the other side of the Danube where we can resume our ride, the third ferry will take us downstream two kilometres and land us on the left side. Left or right.

I know what you're thinking. Previously I've written we'll always choose left, but this time it's definitely right. Not because of any change in political persuasion but neither of us wants to be given 'free' kilometres by a ferry when there's a cycling option.

The Captain welcomes us aboard and smiles broadly. He is a very handsome man, tall with piercing green eyes and curly hair. He asks where we're from and our destination. He's got perfect teeth as well and he speaks two languages. As we dock on the opposite bank, he waves us farewell. Walking down to board the ferry is a beautiful young woman, also smiling and carrying a box of groceries. She wishes us a good day and kisses the Captain. What a handsome couple. Perhaps they'll have tall angular river children who smile at everyone they meet?

As the ferry casts off to return to the far bank, I notice a sign with a cast iron metal plate dangling from it. Attached to the metal plate is a hammer. It's the calling bell for the ferry. I can't help but smile.

The path on this side follows the winding river closely, sometimes almost seeming to float above the surface of the water. Above us are overhanging trees and the steep sided hill is heavy forest with a thick green undergrowth. Large rocks are covered in downy moss. I spend the next few kilometres turning my head from side to side, looking down the river or peering deeply into the forest. Either vista is sensational. We both ride slowly taking in the atmosphere, the scenery, the perfect road hugging the water's edge. It is the best stretch we've encountered on the Danube. There are few cyclists.

A kilometre before Aschach an der Donau there is an small religious memorial attached to an overhanging rock on a bend in the river. I wonder if it's to offer safe passage for barges. At Aschach, crowds of people gather along the Danube shore watching a marching band play tunes on a barge moored a few metres from the bank. The oompa poompa music bounces off the walls of the village. Most of the shops are closed, everyone is watching the band. I notice men in military-style uniforms walking among the crowds. I understand now where the men in Wesenufer were heading. When one band finishes, another one begins. It's a local competition for the best marching band on the Donau. The barge is decorated with pencil pines in huge vases to soften the scaffolding and the military bearing of all these people in red jackets and gold braid.

In the audience are women in elegant boiled-wool jackets and plaid skirts. Their husbands, if not in uniform, are dressed in tweed jackets and pleated trousers with shiny black leather shoes. It's as if we've been transported back to 1959. Young people carry tuba cases almost as big as themselves. A girl with wavy blond hair and blue stockings sits on a bench seat and removes her trumpet from its case. She takes out a cloth and carefully polishes the instrument. Everyone is smiling and enjoying the music while the weather holds.

After the concert, we find an open cafe on the edge of town. It's cosy and warm and as we're only thirty kilometres from Linz we each order a Linzer torte and coffee. As is the tradition in much of Austria, the young waitress serves our coffee on a silver tray accompanied by a glass of water and a digestive biscuit. The sugar spoon is delicately balanced over the steaming coffee. I'm always impressed by this, so civilised and old-worldly. The Linzer torte is reputedly the oldest cake in the world, originating in this region in the late 17th century. I'm not quite sure how one can verify which is the oldest cake? Surely humankind has been baking with flour and sweet fillings for millennium? Perhaps the literature should read 'the oldest recorded recipe of a cake?' I can happily report that this version has a lovely nutty pastry with a rich jam filling and doesn't taste older than twenty-four hours. Delicious.

Refreshed by culture and cake, we cycle along the right bank of the Danube. The land opens up downstream and we're forced to the right of the path by pelotons of racing cyclists on an energetic lunch break from Linz. They are decidedly austere and unfriendly, grinding out the miles with a grim-faced determination. I nod and say hello occasionally, never receiving a response. But I feel I should persist if only to shatter their reverie of time trials and Tour de France glory.

White swans regally float downstream and huge snails attempt to cross the path. With all these bikes, I don't like their chances. We dodge as best we can. We cross the river at the kraftwerk bridge, a power plant and dam operating here since 1974. I read a sign that informs me this plant is the first on the Austrian Danube to use Kaplan turbines with a horizontal shaft. I have no idea what this means, but jot the details into my travel log. You never know when you might share a dinner table with a German engineer who did his or her masters on electricity-generating turbines.

It starts to rain.

We seek shelter in the Casa Grande Cafe an der Donau, an imposing name for a sweet little room filled with brown tables, soft chairs and grey carpet. Fogged windows overlook the river. The lone worker smiles gently and holds up her hands in despair at the weather. We order goulash soup and apple juice. The soup is thick and hearty and I can't resist ordering a second knotty roll to dip into the steaming liquid. It's apparent the rain isn't going to stop so we shrug into our jackets and cycle the remaining ten kilometres into Linz through the outlying suburbs.

We cross the Nibelungen bridge and pedal slowly through the lovely Hautplatz ringed with four-storey buildings and decorated with fountains, ornate lamp-posts and the 'pestsaule' or plague column, erected to remember all those who died in plagues throughout the ages. It's topped with a gold-embossed holy trinity that glistens in the rain. We trundle down the main boulevard, careful to avoid the clattering trams and pedestrians armed with umbrellas.

Despite being the third-largest city in Austria, Linz feels small and accessible with the Linzer Schlosse occupying the high ground above the town. We've booked into the glass encased Austria Trend Schillerpark Hotel, adjoining the casino. It's hardly our style, but we got a very cheap deal. We slop into the immaculate foyer, a trail of water tracing our footsteps. The friendly receptionist shows us where to park our bikes in a locked space in the underground car park. She leads us to our room on the third floor at the end of a very long passageway. Maybe I'm being paranoid but I imagine she wants us as far as possible from the businessmen and women who frequent this establishment.

While Cathie showers, I check the internet connection. It doesn't work. Oh dear. I walk out of the room into the passageway with my computer. The signal improves. I stroll down the passageway and the internet speed increases with each step I take. I close my computer and continue walking to reception to explain the issue to the same worker. To my surprise, she doesn't offer a key to a different room on the same floor. She accompanies me in the lift to the top floor. We step out into a plush foyer and she leads me into a lovely room with a view over the city. She suggests I check the reception in this room. It works perfectly, of course.

She gives me the key. I'm sure this room is much more expensive. She assures me there will be no extra charge and offers to help transport the rest of my luggage. I assure her my wife and I will be able to manage, having only the panniers to carry. I can't wait to show Cathie our room. The receptionist explains that guests on this floor have exclusive use of the lift, which requires keyed access. I'm baffled as to why she didn't just offer us a room closer to the wifi signal downstairs.

Cathie hugs me after she steps into the room. In the bathroom, we have our own sauna and spa and choice of bath or shower. I am especially taken with the full-length glass wall that allows Cathie to sit on our bed and watch me shower. The lucky girl! We wander the space like children in a new playground, trying out all the latest toys. All this for cheaper than a one-star hotel in Australia. We had booked our much cheaper room downstairs for two nights. By a stroke of luck and the good grace of the receptionist, we have the presidential suite all to ourselves for our only rest day on the Danube. I slip into my complimentary bathrobe and gaze across the Linz skyline. The rain thunders down. Ha!

In the evening, we wander the glistening streets of Linz looking for a place to eat. Most establishments are closed. We find a hip restaurant in the Kulture centre but it's booked out so we settle on an all-you-can-eat sushi-train restaurant. The toy train passes with an endless variety of food, from simple sushi and nori rolls to stir-fry chicken and vegetables to quivering desserts of blancmange and bowls of lychees. It's horrendously addictive. We take second helpings of nearly every dish and immediately wish we hadn't. The food is of a quality you'd expect in an all-you-can-eat buffet, but we can't seem to stop eating. Perhaps it's all those miles finally taking their toll.

Back in our suite, my bathrobe feels tighter than it did three hours ago. We sleep in our overly large and comfortable bed, the silent rain running down our double-glazed windows.

The next day, we wander the streets each with a large umbrella, compliments of the hotel. We spend an amusing few minutes admiring a window display of coffee machines from the ages. Each is polished steel or aluminium with valves and metal loops and pressure fittings, all to extract the precious brew.

On the hill, the imposing schloss museum houses everything from tropical fish swimming in a technicolour aquarium to medieval weaponry. I'm agog at the display of weapons - wooden stakes with half-metre blades; chains with spiked metal balls; a double-edged sword with a serrated blade; the innocently named 'war fork' which promises to leave multiple puncture wounds in the chest of your enemy; to simple metre-long spears and clubs.

The next room displays a typical lounge room of 1970's Austria, complete with black and white television, plastic covered space-age lamps and a glass-fronted bar securing bottles of brandy and schnapps. From barbarism to consumerism in a few steps. This is next to a technological exhibition of cars, bicycles, old computers and a video display that allows you to transpose an image of yourself on the opposite wall. For one brief moment in Linz, I am an art exhibition, my curiously distorted figure shadowy and benign on the wall. And then the children from a local school demand their turn at the whiz-bang gadgetry.

Before leaving, I return to some of the paintings on display. One features a naked woman strung up on a crucifix, surrounded by a group of men dressed in gold garments pointing fingers and looking suitably aggressive. One man in the painting holds a large spanner and appears to be attempting to unscrew the woman's nipple. I kid you not. It is most disconcerting. I later learn this was a prime example of the Danube School, a group of artists concentrated in Regensburg, Passau and Vienna who combined a love of dynamic landscapes with a preponderance for depicting the barbaric martyrdoms of the saints.

After this macabre smorgasbord, we retire to a vegetarian restaurant in a lovely old building near the Museum. I order a potato and tofu soup with olive bread. Yes, it sounds uninspiring but is hearty and so delicious I'm tempted to order another bowl. Instead, we both make do with two jugs of bio-beer. I'm not sure what bio-beer is but it tastes so good I order another two pints. And so we drift through the afternoon in a low-ceiling bunker of a room getting slowly sloshed and being ever so pleased that no-one wants to bash our brains out with a mace or tweak our nipples with a medieval spanner. To celebrate our good fortune, on the way back to the hotel we have another Linzer torte - this version is crumbly and buttery with dollops of strawberry jam.

In the evening, we dine at the restaurant in the Kulture house and drink more beer. This could explain why I can't recall what we ate. I remember it was very tasty and we were the oldest people in the restaurant. Everyone else was tall and handsome and immaculately dressed. Women wore scarves and their long hair tumbled over elegant jackets. The men wore tight jeans and were fashionably unshaven. It was as if we'd been transported into a convention of Austrian models. Even the waiters were handsome. We tried to look inconspicious. We were inconspicious!

Accommodation: Austria Trend Hotel Schillerpark, Schillerplatz, Linz. Friendly and helpful staff, wifi, locked storage for bicycles, excellent value, especially if upgraded! My score: 17/20

Restaurant: Gelbes Krokodil, Dametzstrasse 30, Linz. Good quality food in hip surroundings at a very affordable price. Recommended. My score: 17/20.

Vegetarian restaurant: P'aa Restaurant, Altstadt 28, Linz. Good hearty organic food in a lovely old building. My score: 17/20.

Distance cycled: 62 km

Actual distance: 47 km

What I should have said: 'There's a sauna in our hotel room!'

Chapter Fifteen

Linz to Ardagger Markt, Austria

It's no surprise this morning to find the lycra needs to stretch just that little further over my belly. The bigger surprise is that it's not raining. The clouds are indeed high and wispy and we celebrate by quickly riding across the Nibelungen bridge and cycling through parkland on the left bank.

For a rather uninspiring ten kilometres the vista on the far bank is dominated by industrial chimneys smoking constantly, large slag heaps and barges waiting to unload at the docks. During his mad time in power Hitler wanted Linz, his childhood home and one of his favourite places to be the powerhouse of industry.

Despite a wide open river, we have not seen a cruise boat plying its trade along this section. I venture that the passengers are bussed around this uninspiring portion? We arrive in Mauthausen hungry and leg-weary, but before eating we visit the former concentration camp located up a very steep hill just outside of town. The climb is short but difficult and my task is not helped by the jogger who overtakes me on the steepest gradient. Yeah, but he's not carrying panniers, is he! At the top, the fitness fanatic turns around and begins his descent smiling smugly as we pass.

Mauthausen is a bleak grey stone prison that sits rather conspicuously on a hill. Unlike other concentration camps such as Buchenwald that were hidden deep in a forest, this place is clearly visible - its horrible intentions clear to all those who steered along the river. Mauthausen was designated a Grade Three camp intended for political prisoners, or in Nazi-jargon 'the incorrigible political enemies of the Reich.' It quickly gained the macabre nickname of 'knochenmuhle' or bone-grinder. It was used for 'extermination through labour of the intelligentsia'. Prisoners were worked to the point of death on twelve-hour shifts at the nearby granite quarry. Mauthausen was the last camp to be liberated by the Allies in May 1945. It's believed between 122,000 and 320,000 citizens perished during the seven-year existence of this hell hole.

The camp is closed for visitors today so we spend a sombre time gazing up at its bleak and imposing walls and at the guardhouse. We wander around the various memorials near the entrance. Perhaps the most famous inmate was Simon Wiesenthal, who dedicated the rest of his life to hunting down Nazi war criminals. As we hop back on our bikes, the wind blows up from the river like a long and gentle sigh.

We cruise downhill to the village, quiet on this Saturday morning and sit in a cafe for perhaps longer than we should. A local couple next to us ask where we're from and are surprised that two Australians would be so far away from their home, here on the border between Upper and Lower Austria. We explain our trip as best we can. They do what many people have done over the past ten days. They apologise about the weather. We shrug. Today it's not raining.

The next section is lovely with expansive views along the Danube and a well-paved path on a levee to ride upon. Surprisingly, there are few long-distance cyclists. Maybe they transport to Melk along with the cruise passengers?

We cross the river on a dam where the noise of the sluicer releasing water downstream is deafening. For an amusing five minutes I shout obscenities into the breeze and Cathie, standing a few metres away cannot hear a word I say.

Wallsee is a peaceful sleepy town set on a hill on the right bank and dominated by the castle. In the centre of town is a perfectly proportioned church opposite a square with a circular fountain. On either side of the street are red or yellow double-storey buildings with decorative white trim. It's a pristine and handsome little village and we happily complete an extra circuit of the square. A man in an electrician's van watches us and smiles. He chomps down on his sandwich and like us, appreciates the serenity.

At the foot of the town near the river path is a curious statue of a river creature cum wildman dubbed the Donalmandl. Cut from a tree trunk, he has the flowing locks and beard of Neptune and in one giant hand holds a set of spears and in the other a large fish. Disconcertingly, the spears are not tipped with a sharp point but a shape I can only describe as akin to a toilet brush. Perhaps that explains his rather worried and pained expression. A three metre river monster really should not be forced into domestic duties. Scattered around his trunk are numerous round river stones. I like the statue very much and ask Cathie to take a photo of myself beside Donalmandl. Two bearded river men. One a warrior, one a worrier.

We cycle along the flatlands in the river valley among fields of grain. The cycle path is wide and quiet. There are puddles beside the path and everything has the muted tone of a water-logged landscape. Every sound is muffled and dull. The bleak sky reflects a soft light as we trundle into Ardagger Markt. Once again, we are early to our hotel. We pull up outside and a wild-haired man nods hello from the doorway. He is the owner and welcomes us eagerly. It seems as if the weather has scared away many travellers. He's pleased someone has braved the elements to make it to his village. He leads us upstairs to our simple but comfortable room. We enquire whether lunch is still being served. He smiles and in good English says, 'Lunch is always available to guests.'

I have a chicken salad and Cathie has pasta with a creamy asparagus sauce. The asparagus is from the nearby farm and deliciously fresh. We both have a glass of local cider. Afterwards we walk up the hill to the church and cemetery overlooking the town. There's a memorial to those killed in both World Wars and although many of the graves date back to the 19th century, the place is well-maintained with fresh vases of flowers in front of many headstones, even those who died over one hundred years ago.

We walk down the hill and follow the lane to the river. On the main road beside the Danube is a cafe and hotel. We enter through the heavy wooden doors and sit in a booth looking out at the fast-flowing river. A stout woman takes our order - apricot tart and coffee. Despite the increasing chill, we wander out to the back deck and look at the river. Upstream we can see where the Danube has broken its banks and is flooding the low-lying fields. Across the river, an imposing house is surrounded by water, with only a levee keeping the flood from its front door. Tree trunks and debris are washed along on the tide. The newspaper at the bar trumpets the story of local flooding with pictures of inundated houses and villagers walking through knee-deep water in the main street of a nearby town.

We return to the hotel where the owner is sitting at his computer in the light-filled restaurant. He is biting his fingernails anxiously. He calls us over to the computer and explains that he has checked the Donauweg site and it announces that the cycle path is flooded north of here.

At first we don't understand. Surely we can cycle around it on back roads? He explains the prediction is for much worse flooding to come and the Donauweg is expected to be closed all the way to Vienna, three days ride away. An enormous amount of rain has fallen upstream and it's all heading this way in the coming weeks.

'Weeks,' I say, numbly.

'They expect flooding downstream to Bratislava and beyond,' he says.

Our tour to Budapest is sinking, somewhere in the Danube mud.

I picture the towns and villages upstream and remember the photos I saw in the local paper. So much damage, so much heartache and loss for the residents. Our journey is insignificant in the face of this fast-flowing disaster flooding behind us.

'Will your hotel be okay?' I ask.

He nods grimly, 'Ja. We are on high ground at this end of town.' He casts a worried glance through the window in the direction of the river. He doesn't say as much but we understand that some of this village may not escape so easily.

We all sigh heavily. I feel like apologising, but there is nothing that can be said. Cathie and I walk outside and sit under the trees in the courtyard. The owner brings us a beer and leaves us to our thoughts.

We don't speak for a long time, each of us trying to make sense of what we've just been told. The owner said the authorities expect the worst flood in three hundred years in some areas. So much damage.

Reluctantly, we hatch a plan to ride over the hill tomorrow to nearby Amstetten where there is a train that can return us west, away from the Danube. Our journey will have to be postponed, perhaps until our next trip to Europe. We both agree we've enjoyed Germany and Austria immensely. We can't help but feel sad to think of all the riverside towns we've cycled through, now under threat from the deluge.

The English-language media informs us that Passau is at this very moment experiencing its worst flood in five hundred years and much of the town, at the confluence of three rivers, is under water. Lives have been lost and the town evacuated. I recall how we wandered the streets in glorious sunshine only a few days ago, all the young people sitting in parks beside the river basking in the warmth of an imminent summer. It's unbelievably sad.

We have a quiet dinner in the hotel. We are the only guests. The owner nods as we tell him our plans to return, perhaps in a year to complete our journey. He smiles grimly, 'We will be here, I hope.'

Accommodation: Gasthoff Hotel Schiffsmeisterhaus, Markt 65, Ardagger Markt. Friendly hosts, storage for bikes, wifi, small but comfortable rooms. My score: 16/20

Restaurant: Gasthoff Hotel Schiffsmeisterhaus Restaurant. Ample servings for lunch or dinner, traditional hearty food, good value. Local cider available. My score 15/20.

Distance cycled: 62 km

Actual distance: 56 km

What I should have said: 'I don't suppose you have a boat big enough to carry two overweight Australians and their bicycles?'

Chapter Sixteen

Ardagger Markt to Grein, Austria

As we waited for our flight home to Australia, I read of the damage inflicted on the numerous lovely towns and villages along the Danube, all the way to Bratislava. It was indeed heartbreaking for many locals. We had spent a quiet few days in Paris, feeling somehow guilty that as tourists we can easily cycle through the paradise of Europe and just as easily escape should the weather or natural disasters intrude. It's not so simple for those who live on the Danube. We hoped that no further lives would be lost in the tumult.

As our plane flew over Europe, I looked down to the green and vast land below. The route map showed we were 30,000 feet somewhere above Hungary. I tried to scan the horizon for the Danube, wondering if the flood had reached all the way to Budapest. All I could see were fields and forests and the occasional town before cloud cover obscured my view. I swallowed hard and made a vow to return and finish our journey to the Hungarian capital sometime in the following year. Perhaps the best response of tourists such as ourselves is to return and help the local economies to recover. I recall only a few weeks ago riding along the upper Danube and seeing children playing in a shallow harmless stream.

On returning home, I scoured the online newspapers for news. A dike had failed near Deggendorf and much of the town had been covered by two metres of surging water. Photos showed rescue teams in power boats saving people from roofs in Passau, the water flooding up to the second-storey of many houses. A mess of cars had been picked up by the flood and slammed together into a pile of junk. A family in a canoe paddle along what was once a crowded and busy motorway.

The power of nature is something we ignore at our peril.

Over a year later, at the turn of the season in September, Cathie and I are once again sitting in the courtyard of the hotel in Ardagger Markt. We have recently completed a long cycle tour from St Malo in France to Prague in the Czech Republic - over 2,500 kilometres through five European countries - which will be the subject of another book.

We have travelled by train from Prague to Amstetten with Jenny and Craig to complete our Danube adventure. Although we have spent the past forty days in the saddle crossing Europe, we couldn't leave this trip unfinished.

Unfortunately, the owner is not present today. We order a beer and sit under the vines in the courtyard. It is a sunny Autumn day of twenty degrees. There is a conference taking place at the hotel. Well-dressed business-people file out from a side room and head towards the two tables of cakes and coffee. I'd like to join them, but we're really not dressed for the occasion. The hotel looks fresher than I remember. Perhaps it's had a makeover in the winter. It certainly seems as though business is going well. I'm pleased for the owner, but disappointed that he's not here. I would like to ask him how the village has recovered after last year's deluge.

We hop back on our bikes and head towards the Danube. Our first view of the river this year is vastly different from our last sighting the previous year. Today the Danube is a benign and pleasant stream seemingly incapable of ferocity and menace. Birds flit above the calm surface and two swans float regally downstream. The Donauweg is quiet and serene. We say goodbye to Ardagger Markt and silently wish it a bright future.

The ride to Grein is over a bridge undergoing repair, perhaps from the damage of the high wasser? We cruise into town and are once again struck by how prosperous Austria is. People in casual clothes sit in outdoor cafes and enjoy the late afternoon sun and cheesecake.

We check into our hotel which has a huge garage for bicycles including a substantial set of tools for the use of guests. I spy a hose and consider giving Craig a quick wash. The owner explains it's only for bike shoes, not bikes. I don't quite understand why anyone would want to wash their shoes with a high pressure hose until I ask her about access to the laundry. She explains that it is out of order because a cyclist put his shoes in the washing machine. Oh well, Craig will have to be satisfied with a quick brush and my clothes can luxuriate in the bathroom sink, yet again.

I'm enormously impressed with the set of lycra the hotel offers for sale on a mannequin at the front entrance. The shirt is a cross between a traditional Austrian lederhosen-style top with braiding and elaborate decoration and the chequerboard red and white of the Croatian flag. The shorts are black with flower decorations. It's what all fashionable Austrian cyclists are wearing this season. I'm not sure what Craig, or indeed Cathie would think if I fronted up to breakfast in this outfit but it's tempting to find out.

Cathie and I take a slow walk around town. We enter the church through a heavy wooden door to be met by sterile glass sliding doors that open as we step forward. It's cool and dark inside. We walk to the altar which is backed by statues of two gold-robed priests looking down from up high. The altar is currently decorated with ornamental wheat, barley and corn motifs, in the hope of a bountiful harvest. The pews remind me of primary school with a heavy wooden desk to lean upon while praying. There's even a hole for an inkwell near the centre aisle. Cathie tells me not to be so disrespectful. We try to leave via the same doors. The sliding glass won't open. We're trapped with the priests and memories of unhappy school years. Cathie spies the red button near a pew which magically opens the doors and allows heathens like me to escape the clutches of our Lord.

In a gilded cage outside the church is Jesus as a child looking down at robed men lying on the rocks. I imagine they are the three wise men. Someone has thrown a beer bottle through the cage so it appears as if the wise ones have hit the turps and are sleeping off the repercussions.

We walk to the river where a cruise ship is berthed. White-coated waiters work below deck in the kitchen. We spy them through the tiny portholes. They appear to be laboriously adding ice to empty glasses, perhaps soon to be filled with punch for the passengers who are walking gingerly down the gang plank, welcomed by a dapper member of the crew.

It's 6pm. I imagine they've been transported somewhere during the day - to a castle or a hilltop town - anywhere to escape the boredom of the Danube at 8 kph.

The restaurant next to the boat is offering a three-course special for the princely sum of 7.50 Euro. How can we resist? We climb the stairs and take a seat near the window. Now we can watch the rich passengers as they dine. In turn, we eat a delicious home-style meal of pancake soup, fish and potatoes and a simple apricot tart. It's probably nothing like what our friends are eating on board, but it's very tasty and served by a gentle old lady in a white and pale blue dress who quickly refills my beer glass as soon as it's empty.

The white-coated waiters aboard start mingling among the guests with hor d'oeuvres, served on a silver tray. Cathie and I finish our apricot tart.

'What's the difference between a canape and a hor d'oeuvre?' I ask.

Cathie suppresses a giggle, 'Or an amuse bouche,' she says.

'A what?'

'It's like a canape ...'

'Or a hor d'oeuvre,' I add.

'Only it's served in restaurants before the start of the meal,' Cathie says.

'It's a freebie!' I say.

'Exactly,' she says.

'Then I prefer an amuse bouche,' I say.

'Cheapskate,' she responds.

We look across at the passengers. They are daintily choosing another canape, or hor d'oeuvre from the tray.

'What's the difference between freeloaders and celebrities,' I ask.

Cathie rolls her eyes and signals for the bill.

Accommodation: Pension Martha, Haupstrasse, Grein. Clean, comfortable rooms with a very friendly hosts. Garage and tools for bicycles and a self-serve cafe for coffee, wine and beer. Excellent breakfast. My score: 17/20

Restaurant: Schinakel Inn. On the waterfront at the main pier of Grein. Wonderful views. Simple tasty food without pretension. Great value. Watch how the other half live while you dine. My score: 14/20.

Distance cycled: 33 km (and a train trip from the Czech Republic)

What I should have said: 'Of course, we're passengers, Captain. How can you doubt us?'

Chapter Seventeen

Grein to Melk, Austria

A smart hotel knows the importance of a customer departing the next morning in a positive mood. Cue the perfect breakfast.

'Would you like another egg, perhaps? More coffee?'

I wait until my mouth is not full of food to answer. I've said it before but yoghurt and fresh fruit make an excellent start to any breakfast. Followed by a boiled egg; ham; a selection of cheeses; brown bread and a choice of espresso or filter coffee. The hotel caters for cyclists and we all seem to have a large appetite. The room this morning is crowded with lycra and gluttons. I don't have to push too many people away from the smorgasbord.

To cap our pleasant morning departure, the host gives me a small spray pack of deodorant for free. I'm not sure if she's suggesting I smell or just being kind. Let's agree it's the latter although the former is undoubtedly true.

We cycle away, smelling sweetly with contented and full stomachs. It's a cool morning with the mist shouldering the hills on either side of the Danube. The cruise boat from last night has departed. The blue Danube looks pea green today and seems to be in a particularly sombre mood. Not us. I feel like singing. No hills, no rain and we maintain a much faster pace than on our recent passage across five countries from France to the Czech Republic where the hills were alive with the sound of heavy breathing.

The autumn trees are fanciful orange and quilt the hills intermingled with dark green firs. We've been waiting for autumn across the continent and it's finally arrived with a blaze of colour and fallen leaves that caress our tyres.

We cross the Ybbs-Persenbeug kraftwerk, admiring as always

the geometry of simple lines that make this river machinery so appealing. A barge enters the lock as we cycle above on the pathway. A young man in a heavy overcoat and a black beanie is casting a fishing line from the kraftwerk into the river below. The hook has a long way to travel before it plops into the water. I wonder how he hopes to haul a fish up fifty metres of wriggling air?

Ybbs an der Donau is a town of yellow buildings beginning with a particularly impressive therapeutic establishment. On the roof of the nearby kitchen and laundry, three men are replacing the slate tiles amid billowing clouds of steam rising through the gaps in the ceiling. It looks rather dangerous and suitably Gothic for a town that was established over one thousand years ago.

Ybbs also has a bicycle museum, closed today. We notice old rusting frames of bikes at strategic parts of the town advertising the museum. They make me smile. As does the excellent cheese pocket and espresso we order from the backerei.

The mist has lifted from the hills and the Danube seems wider and more free-flowing with the open sky above. The path is smooth and largely free of other cyclists. I imagine all our fellow diners at breakfast have headed upstream. We cruise into Emmersdorf where our pension is located. I'm astonished when I glance at my watch and discover it's only midday. Oh dear.

We take a chance and sheepishly ring the doorbell. A smiling dark-haired woman opens the door, surprised at our arrival. She speaks limited English, but seems to understand she's dealing with Australians who can't tell the time. She shows us through the downstairs gym and dance studio and leads us to our first floor room at the front which has a lovely view over the majestic Melk Abbey. We explain through mime and poor German that we'd like to leave our bags here and cycle across the bridge to Melk before returning to properly check in this afternoon. She agrees.

We learn she's originally from Romania and Cathie mentions Maramures County, one of our favourite parts of Europe. The woman positively beams when we tell her we were there four years ago. That is her homeland and she's justly proud of its beauty. I wrote a travel article for a Sydney newspaper on the tall-steepled churches of Maramures. They are truly amazing. The church interior is often no bigger than a large living room of a suburban house and yet the steeples are among the tallest wooden church structures in the world. I remember stepping back and back and back to try to get the whole steeple into my camera view. I ended up falling into a ditch.

And now we're off to visit a church of an entirely different kind. The famous baroque monastery known as Melk Abbey. Viewed from the highway, it resembles an apricot-coloured ocean liner marooned on a hill. We cycle towards it from the river, past the numerous cruise boats berthing three-deep at the wharf to unload busloads of tourists and pilgrims.

Today lower Melk resembles East Brooklyn, crowded as it is with American tourists in baseball caps and sensible shoes, eating hot dogs and drinking beer. We join the throng at a restaurant on the square and have a tasty lunch of pork belly and sauerkraut. The twang of voices echoes off all this ancient stone.

And so to the Abbey. Built in the early 18th century it's a baroque masterpiece of countless frescoes and gold sculptures and most impressive of all - a library that houses numerous manuscripts from medieval times. The monks regarded the library as second only to the church and the design of the Abbey reflects this, with the left side given over to the Marble Hall linked to the right-sided library by a semi-circular balcony offering spectacular views down the Danube. A hush falls over the crowd as we enter the library. Floor to ceiling ancient manuscripts line the walls. In glass cases are documents dating from 570 to the 18th century. I am in awe.

Dear reader, you may be viewing this book on an electronic device that can store thousands of documents, but nothing can compare or replace the sheer beauty and majesty of a well-stocked library. All that history. All that knowledge. This room in the Abbey is my church, my cathedral. I don't want to leave but the guard begins to look at me suspiciously. She knows I want to reach out and touch the manuscripts. To feel the pulse of ancient scribes.

We continue on to the magnificent high baroque church. An excess of gold braid and elaborate frescoes, it's a marvellously over-the-top place of worship. I don't know where to look next. At the gold angel; the clothed skeleton in a crypt with a quill pen between his fingers or at the triumphal gold sculptures above the altar of Peter and Paul shaking hands, joined in their martyrdom with the inscription, 'without a legitimate battle, there is no victory.'

So important was this Abbey and such was its esteem, that it managed to survive the ravages of the Napoleonic Wars and the demonic reign of Hitler. It now stands regal and timeless on a rock beside the Danube. Long may it remain.

With the number of American tourists, I'm rather amused to see the current exhibition in the adjoining rooms to the Abbey. One contains a black-cloth draped sculpture that, according to the nearby sign, is a tribute to the courage and actions of two modern-day whistleblowers, Edward Snowden and Chelsea Manning. The sculpture treats them as heroes, as indeed do I. The American tourist may think differently. Mr Snowden is currently exiled in Russia while Chelsea Manning is serving life in prison in the USA for treason. One man's treason is another man's fight for freedom.

We take our politics out to the lovely ornamental gardens and the mauve coloured building that contains a cafe and numerous pastel murals. We can't decide between the apricot marillenkuchen and the nutty chocolate kolomanitorte, so we order both. We're the only people in the cafe. It's a little disconcerting eating from a mirror topped table. My nose hair doesn't make for a pleasing appetiser to the torte.

We cycle back to the pension in the late afternoon, over the cobblestones of sleepy Emmersdorf. I'm pleased to be on this side of the river, looking across at Melk Abbey, sturdy and resolute on the far shore.

Accommodation: Pension Egger, Emmersdorf. Friendly hosts, large rooms with a view of Melk Abbey, wifi, a gym if you feel so inclined, good breakfast, garage for bicycles. My score: 16/20

Dinner: Felsengart Heurigenschenke, Emmersdorf. A welcoming wood panelled dining room with a view to Melk Abbey. The food is cheap and plentiful with an excellent pumpkin soup and huge serves of typical Austrian schnitzels. My score: 15/20

Distance cycled: 61 km

What I should have said: 'Anybody here vote for Obama?'

Chapter Eighteen:

Melk to Tulln, Austria

I've never eaten breakfast in a gym before, but it's a lovely spread and our host Elli explains that she leases the pension out in the winter months for groups who demand such things as gym equipment and floor-to-ceiling mirrors for dance classes. She tells us her musician husband and children live not far from the pension, with their two horses and twenty-five chickens. She brings us some boiled eggs, as if to prove their existence. She's a lovely shy woman who understands the needs of travellers and responds accordingly. We feel privileged to have stayed here.

This morning alternates between bright sunshine and heavy cloud. We trundle along the north side of the Danube through sleepy villages until we reach Willendorf, with its simple stone houses of green wooden shutters and terraced vineyards rising from the river. Willendorf is where in 1908, while excavating a home site, a local man found a curious ten centimetre tall statuette of a female figure. Scientific tests on the figure showed it to be somewhere between 25,000 and 28,000 years old. Dubbed 'the Venus of Willendorf,' it's believed the figure is a fertility goddess due to the emphasis on her large breasts and vulva. The figure was carved during the Paleolthic period from limestone and tinted with red ochre. She also goes by the nickname of 'la poire' due to her distinct pear shape. Curiously, she has no feet and no discernible facial features. The original figure now is housed in Vienna, but a model remains in Willendorf near the site of her discovery a century ago.

Craig begins groaning as we leave the village. I don't know what he's got to complain about, having slept the night in a musician's studio amongst a vast array of instruments and recording equipment. His moans seem to be coming from the front wheel, the one that was repaired only two weeks ago. I decide to ignore it until Budapest.

At Spitz, the rain starts spitting - sorry, I couldn't resist - even though the sun is shining. There's nothing I enjoy more than a sun shower while cycling. Cool and refreshing. Spitz is also the location of where Cathie had her first taste of Austrian food six years ago when we were driving across the continent from Istanbul. It was not a pleasant introduction. The words 'dog food' were perhaps a little harsh to describe what was offered, but only a little. Happily, we now know what to order and love the heavy teutonic dishes.

The car ferry at Spitz is a cumbersome looking vessel that has wooden planks on the top deck where one car is parked. As it sets off from the dock, I wonder how the car gets off the boat. It doesn't appear to have the usual roll-on roll-off docking mechanism of most cross river ferries. And the gangplank on the opposite bank looks too narrow for a vehicle. We sit in the sunshine and watch. Of course, the car rolls off quite easily and snugly fits between the guard rails as it slowly climbs the gangplank. Did we really believe the industrious Austrians would not plan everything so precisely?

The vineyards sloping up from the river are yellow and orange as the leaves change with the season. Yet there are still heavy bunches of grapes on the vine? A group of pickers move along in rows expertly removing the ripe fruit. I imagine it's for sweet wine, being so late in the season. I stop and pick a grape. It's not as sweet as I expected. My guess? Riesling.

The next village of Durnstein is a town with everything. Craggy cliffs; castle ruins high among the rocks; a delightful light blue church with white statues; a sandy beach on the Danube for bathing; an ancient wall around part of the village; a wharf with a cruise boat and a swarm of Japanese tourists getting off the boat as two Australian cyclists ride past. The tourists stop taking photos of the castle ruins and start snapping the ruin of an old Australian riding a bicycle. I'm a little chuffed and so offer a friendly wave and nearly run over a old Japanese man looking the wrong way. An International incident is averted by centimetres and we both continue sheepishly on our way. The old man to a cafe and me to a bench seat further downstream where I can admire the beauty of Durnstein in relative safety.

Although the castle is in ruins it has quite a history having been the jail of Richard the Lionheart during the Third Crusade. He was eventually freed by decree of the Pope although he was then handed over to Emperor Henry 6th. And now the town is a stopover for cycle and boat tourists who sample the local wine and take a hundred happy snaps of the craggy ruins. Such is the way of all history.

We stop for cheesecake and coffee in Stein. Although we ask for a cappuccino, the waitress brings two mugs groaning under an explosion of cream. I spoon the cream onto my cheesecake and sip the excellent coffee. We sit on the cafe balcony overlooking the pretty town square somewhat burdened with too many car parking spaces. Instead of admiring simple yet elegant buildings, we watch the old man try to park an Audi.

'I wish he'd run over Craig so I could claim the insurance,' I say.

'And how will you get to Budapest without Craig,' Cathie says.

'I'd buy a shiny new replacement.'

'You'd hate it within a day.'

'No I wouldn't,' I say, 'You're just worried I'd go too fast for you.'

'You already do, even on an old clunker like Craig.'

'You see, even you think he's useless,' I add.

'Ssshhh, he can hear you.'

'Good!'

We wander somewhat hesitantly through the cobblestone back streets of Stein and its partner town of Krems an der Donau. There are too many shoppers and the lanes are narrow, so progress is slow and Craig is groaning even more. I suspect he heard our cafe conversation.

After Krems, the river valley opens out and we cycle along a wide path with the wind behind us and a cruise boat ahead. We follow the boat for an hour. I can't believe how fast it's going. We average 20 kph and yet fail to bridge the gap.

Finally we give up and stop for lunch at a riverside restaurant near the town of Traismauer. The garden has topiary trees and mass plantings of hydrangeas, their bulbous flowers wilting in the sun. We sit at an outdoor table and order two plates of goulash with extra bread. I'm surprised by the number of diners indoors. The restaurant seems isolated, but it's in a pleasant location between a small marina and the Danube with long views up and down the river.

A group of four people sit near us with their large dogs on leashes. The dogs look thirsty and tired. The owners order beer and the youngest woman goes inside and returns with a large bowl full of water for the pets. They lap it up thirstily then go to sleep under the table. I know how they feel.

After lunch we cycle alongside the river on a levee with a swamp on one side amid the scraggily bush. On a downhill path, I almost run over a tiny snake. I'm surprised it's still active so late in the year. Ten minutes later, Cathie and I both dodge a large sleeping yellow-belly black snake. I hate snakes. Two hundred metres ahead, an old man cycles towards me. I call out 'snake, serpent' not knowing what the German word is for the reptile. I wiggle my arm elaborately in the air. The man looks at me as if I'm offering him free belly dance lessons on a bicycle. He passes, giving me a wide berth.

I hope he saw the snake.

I hope he doesn't report me to the police.

The entry to our overnight stop of Tulln is rather bland with power lines arching over ploughed fields. We cycle through non-descript villages before turning back onto the Danube. The sign to Tulln directs us to a splendid three-way bridge over a sparkling pond before we enter an imposing square with a rathaus resembling a large wedding cake - white icing with delicate mauve decoration. The town looks wealthy and content. It's even installed an underground car park in the square which boasts numerous outdoor cafes. Cafes on top, cars below. As it should be.

Our pension for the night is down a back street near the centre of town. A young woman meets us and shows us the locked cage where we can put Craig and Jenny. I get an unusual amount of pleasure from locking him behind bars for the evening. I feel sorry for Jenny.

We wander the streets of Tulln in the evening and decide to eat at the Gasthaus Goldene Schiff on recommendation of the pension owner. When the waiter arrives I ask for the menu and he explains that food is not served until 6pm. We are a little early because I wanted a beer. The table behind us is already eating. I'm about to say something but notice Cathie shaking her head, just slightly. I order a beer instead.

'What was that all about?' I ask.

'It's a funeral,' she says.

'What. In a pub?'

She rolls her eyes. 'They've obviously all been to a funeral and this is the wake. That's why they got served early. You fool.'

A priest walks into the room and hugs each of the diners. I'm pleased my wife is smarter than me.

When we finally are allowed to order, the food is delicious.

Accommodation: Pension Kirchenblick, Tulln. Friendly staff, good wifi, big rooms, large breakfast, close to the town centre. My score: 16/20

Dinner: Gasthaus Goldenes Schiff, WienerStrasse 10, Tulln. An award-winning restaurant that serves excellent food in a friendly convivial atmosphere. My score: 16/20

Distance cycled: 80 km

What I should have said: 'My condolences.'

Chapter Nineteen:

Tulln to Vienna, Austria

It's raining quite heavily this morning, which seems appropriate as our last attempt to cycle to Vienna was thwarted by the tragic floods of 2013. However a little dampness shall not deter us this time. The morning ride begins with shades of dark green - the road and rail bridge we cross is painted in a military tone, the Danube is decidedly pea-soup in colour and the trees on the bank are dark and bleak. On the south bank is a row of low hills cloaked in heavy cloud. We stick to the north bank on a straight wide path atop a levee, dodging the numerous slugs and scaring birds from their hides.

On the safe side of the levee are rows of small brown wooden houses on stilts. They are impossibly cute, like cubby houses for adults. Most are perfectly square with one side section open as a verandah, just large enough to fit a few chairs and a table. They have wooden shutters on the windows and I'm inclined to believe they're holiday houses for Vienna residents keen on fishing. The gardens don't have fences and the whole place has a jaunty 'free-from-care' appearance, even in the cold rain.

I don't mind cycling in the rain. I have my waterproof jacket with a hood and I recall a famous Dutch saying when people complain about going outside in the rain. 'You are not made of sugar.' Lovely and so very Dutch.

The only thing that frustrates me about cycling in the rain is how to keep my feet dry. I have tried everything. Four pairs of 'waterproof' shoe covers; SealSkinz 'waterproof' socks and even plastic bags tied at the ankles. You'll note by my judicious use of inverted commas that nothing has been successful. This morning, my latest pair of shoe covers are saturated within twenty minutes and I sigh heavily, ready for a squelching ride into Vienna.

The river is slow and wide and predictably no-one is cycling along the path so Cathie and I resign ourselves to the task and enjoy the scenery. Swans and ducks and hills and I wonder how long this rain will persist?

At Korneuburg, we decide its time to dry off in a cafe and eat cake. The first backerei we come to is perfect with the heating on high and an excellent pumpkin cake and coffee. We sit at a window seat and watch the rain tumble down.

'Ten minutes and we'll go,' I venture.

'If it's stopped raining,' says Cathie.

We watch the old ladies coming in, folding their umbrellas carefully, placing them neatly in the stand beside the door.

'Aaahhh, it hasn't stopped yet,' I say.

'Let's wait until 11:15 and we'll go no matter what,' Cathie answers.

In the cafe bathroom, I hold my shoe covers under the electric hand dryer. Water sprays across the mirror. I wipe it with a paper hand towel.

'We'll definitely leave at 11:30,' Cathie says when I return to the table.

I pay the bill and sigh. It's 11:45 and we have no choice.

The rain is bucketing down and we dodge puddles and nervous Audi drivers as we make our way back to the river. The path leads through a lovely green pasture with a stand of yellow trees. There's not a soul about. It's hard to believe we're less than ten kilometres from a major European city. We relax and listen to the distant hub of truck tyres on wet roads from somewhere through the bush.

A lone skyscraper emerges from the tumult.

Vienna.

As if on cue, the signs announcing the Euro Velo 6 stop

appearing, just when we need them to navigate through the various cycle paths on offer. We attempt to keep as close as possible to the river but get lost in a maze of office buildings and a new development called Donau City - numerous apartment blocks and office towers joined by wide wind-swept pedestrian boulevards. People parachute behind unwieldly umbrellas as I consult a new app I bought a few nights ago that tells me where I am on a map. I will never be lost again. Well, not for long. The app works a treat even on a wet screen and we see, rather disconcertingly, that Vienna is a very big city and our pension is somewhere - check of app - over there.

We cross the Danube and head into a maze of muscular yet stately buildings. The Vienna bike infrastructure is extremely good. If we're not cycling down an allocated centre section of wide boulevards, we're at least given a well-marked bike path away from the traffic. For six kilometres, we circle the city streets, consulting the app, looking up at the lovely imposing buildings and dodging the splashes from trucks. It occurs to me as I pass yet another row of ornate stone buildings that we have entered the realm of an Imperial power, long since dethroned, but Vienna continues to remind us all of just how much wealth, power and culture was centred on this small patch of ground beside the Danube.

I've been to Vienna twice before. As a tourist, I'm agog at the sights but the city appears as from another era - elegant memories and faded glories that loom ever larger as the present shrinks in a miasma of neon franchises and featureless office buildings. It's past is beautiful, but unlike Paris - a city that seems to constantly reinvent itself with energy and creativity - Vienna is frozen in its stately history, a beautifully-preserved relic of refinement and majesty that remains apart from the modern world. A museum, a mute cathedral, a broad-shouldered apartment block, a cobbled laneway - a ghost wind blows down the Danube.

Our pension is near the Mariahilfer Strasse, touted as the place to go shopping in Vienna. Why people regard shopping as pleasurable activity is beyond my feeble comprehension. This street looks no different from a thousand shopping centres in a thousand different cities in the world, scarred with labels and neon and big-lipped wafer-thin models on twenty-metre billboards promising nothing more than a large credit card bill and an empty feeling in the stomach. Or the soul.

We check into our pension, wash our muddy clothes and bodies and get dressed before heading out for a very late lunch. There's a warm friendly Italian restaurant on the corner. What food is more welcoming when you're hungry than Italian? Pizza, pasta and beer.

We set off to visit our favourite sites of the city. They are not shopping malls.

We take the U-bahn a few stops across town to St Stephen's Cathedral, the seat of the Archbishop of Vienna and a Romanesque and Gothic fortress immediately recognisable from a distance by its multi-coloured tiled roof, reminiscent of many buildings in the French city of Beaune. Built in the 14th century, it houses the tomb of the Holy Roman Emperor, Frederick 3rd in a red marble medieval sarcophagus that began to be constructed twenty-five years before he died. Frederick was certain of both his resting place and his role in history.

Last time we visited St Stephen's, there was a wonderfully exotic interior light show that owed more to the psychedelic 1960s than medieval religion. It was a whirl of rainbow colours and flashes. I loved it. Tonight, the interior is bathed in more sombre tones, but I'm pleased to see the LSD flavour has been retained for the exterior light show. The bells begin ringing at 7pm. The story goes that Beethoven knew he was profoundly deaf when he saw the pigeons flying from the towers when the bells rang and yet he could not hear them. St Stephen's has the largest bell in Austria, so dear

Ludwig was certain of his fate. Tonight the crowds content themselves with gelato and photos of the church where Mozart was married and where his funeral was held in 1791 after his tragic death at the young age of thirty-five.

We walk across town to look at the art of our other favourite son of Vienna, the architect Otto Wagner. Wagner was a professor at the Vienna School of Art and was responsible for the training of a generation of Viennese Art Nouveau disciples who created many of the beautiful buildings of the city. Wagner himself designed a number of wonderful buildings including the Postal Savings Building that houses a Wagner exhibition and the deceptively elegant Karlsplatz Station. The whimsical paintings and balconies of Wagner's Majolica House never fails to make me smile.

From the medieval to the majestic, it's time for dinner. We wander through the Stadthof precinct where muscular buildings face off at one hundred metres, each one fronted by a King on a horse brandishing a weapon. It's all very battle hungry and old world Imperial.

The Museum Quarter has been redeveloped into a hive of art galleries and restaurants and Halle is probably the pick of places to eat. It's Friday night and we haven't booked but a friendly waiter sits us opposite the lift, exactly where we sat last year. We must look dishevelled enough to be exiled to this corner. I don't mind. The food is inexpensive and tasty, the waiters friendly and there's a woman who wears low-slung jeans in a rather butch fashion and always seeems to be making a scene of some sort with the staff, of whom I think she is their boss. Tonight she attempts to close a curtain. It fails to move. She pulls it with an almighty swing and it rips, naturally. She quickly secures it behind a bench seat and moves away. Tomorrow, it's someone else's problem.

We make a toast to Beethoven, Mozart, Wagner and those dudes on horse leading the charge.

Outside the rain has stopped and the sky is a lovely shade of regal blue.

Accommodation: Pension Pharmador, Schottenfeldgasse 39, Vienna. Friendly staff, garage for bicycles, good wifi, breakfast included and within twenty minutes walk of many of the sites of the city. My score: 15/20

Dinner: Halle Cafe-Restaurant, Museumplatz 1, Vienna. Inexpensive creative food that isn't heavy or traditional. Some people complain the staff are rude. Not in my experience. Great building and lively atmosphere. Open till 2 am, if that takes your fancy, although I prefer the lunch special. My score: 15/20

Distance cycled: 48km

What I should have said: 'Why does the curtain need to be closed?'

Chapter Twenty:

Vienna, Austria to Bratislava, Slovakia

We make an early morning escape from Vienna before the city has a chance to wake and realise that it's a stupendously perfect Saturday of blue sky and gentle wind. Not even the clang of a tram can distract me from enjoying the wide open unpopulated boulevards of this regal city. We old people know when we're at our best, early in the day before the excesses wear us down. Even Craig is quiet and happy.

We cycle onto the Donauinsel, a magical twenty-one kilometre island in the Danube, the lungs and pulse of Vienna. Ringed with walking tracks, bicycle paths, autumn trees and restful views of the Vienna skyline, it's the perfect start to the day. I imagine living in Vienna would be much easier with the presence of this bicycle playground. Our only companions this morning are the occasional jogger and singing birds.

We make do with ten kilometres on the paths before crossing to the north side of the river and following a quiet track along a levee for two glorious hours. I pass the time by counting the vapour trails of planes criss-crossing Europe. It hardly seems like we've exerted any energy before we arrive at Orth an der Donau, a town with a four-towered medieval castle; a pink Baroque church and exceptionally yummy cheese pastries at the local cafe. I also order a cappuccino with cream. When it arrives I spoon the cream onto my pastry and drink the hot black coffee. Cathie watches, horrified.

'I get coffee-flavoured cream for my cake and don't have to pay any extra,' I explain.

She shakes her head in disbelief, but I know she's tempted to do the same.

'Mmmmmm, coffee and cream,' I say.

The surface of the path on the levee deteriorates after Orth, but it's still a wonderfully easy ride, with ponds, forest and farmlands either side of us. In the late morning, we arrive in Hainburg, a handsome town four kilometres from the Slovak border on a bend in the Danube, with castle ruins on a prominent hill and an onion-dome church. We're tempted to stop for lunch until Cathie says, 'Breakfast in Vienna, lunch in Bratislava.'

We both smile.

Coming from a vast country surrounded by ocean, we are thrilled by the opportunity to cycle from one capital city to the next between meals.

Of course there has also been a much more significant divide between these two cities in the recent past. Less than a generation ago, Slovakia and much of Eastern Europe was imprisoned behind a seemingly impenetrable wall of dogma and defence, yet a wall that proved to be built not so much by stone, iron and barbed wire but by the clenched fist of power and certainty.

Once the Gorbachov-enlightened phase of glasnost offered a promise of freedom and modernity, until all certainty was swept aside. Yet many would argue that once the wall's defences were breached it wasn't the Eastern prisoners who were rushing to escape but the shysters and opportunists of the West who saw new markets to exploit and conquer, not with the gun but with the shiny promise of unlimited credit and instant wealth.

The Mercedes replaced the Trabant; neon advertising replaced Party announcements and freedom could be measured by how many people you could exploit in the name of success.

I don't for a moment believe anyone in Slovakia wants to go back to the days of bread lines and State control, but I also wonder how many people long for a time where employment was guaranteed, where women didn't have to sell themselves to the obscenity of pornography and where majestic cities like Bratislava were not turned into old-town tourist parks for wealthy foreigners.

But, I digress.

Cathie and I crest a hill in Austria and are dumbfounded by the vision a few kilometres in front of us. A fortress-like row of high-rise apartment blocks dominate the hill north of the Danube on the outskirts of Bratislava. After so many kilometres of nothing but forest and village, it's a shock to the system. To the right, high on a cliff sits Bratislava Castle, a much more appealing motif for the town.

We pedal slowly over the futuristic New Bridge, nicknamed the UFO, which is now littered with graffiti on both its bicycle lanes. We've been to Bratislava before and know just where to head once the bridge spits us into the Old Town.

Cafe Stur is perhaps one of our favourite cafes in Europe. Located on a small square near the historic entry to the old town, it offers delicious salads, cakes and coffee at inexpensive prices. Free wifi, honey mead, ginger lemonade, banana-caramel cake ... need I go on. We celebrate our 'breakfast-lunch in two capital cities' with a spinach quiche, salad, beer and raspberry cheesecake.

It's nice to be back in Bratislava. The old town is quite small and very accessible - you could walk around it in an hour, including a climb up the back alleys to the Castle. Most streets are filled with cafes and restaurants, with some in hidden enclaves under old buildings in cellars or down cobblestone alleys. The town square has a lovely bunch of ornate buildings, but I cannot shake the feeling of being in an old-world tourist park. This lovely and endearing section of Bratislava seems to be no longer a place where people live, but now entirely given over to hotels, restaurants and souvenir shops.

As if to reinforce this view, on the next street corner a film is being shot. The roadway is closed as scores of workers run around to ready a scene where an old tram and a Mercedes collide. I'm struck by how many people it takes to shoot one short scene in a movie - there must be fifty people working here from the director and photographer in their chairs studying the most recent shot to the six security men in red shirts at each exit point, to the lighting workers and caterers. Somewhere amongst this rabble, there are actors waiting their cue.

At the very next street corner we come across a wedding party about to enter a church. The bride is radiant in a sleeveless white frock, her red hair pulled back tightly in an elegant bun, her father in a grey suit - equal parts proud and nervous, I imagine. The guests wait in a grassy courtyard. From a wooden bridge above them, tourists train their cameras on the scene.

Everyone can be the star in their own movie, at least once in our lives.

Bratislava is the only capital that borders two countries - Austria and Hungary. I wonder if the residents of all those tower blocks we saw on arrival work in Slovakia or commute daily west to Vienna or east to Hungary? While thinking of this, I almost step in front of a red tram. The bell sounds and I decide to stop thinking about the past or future of this lovely town and instead to go and drink a beer at a outdoor bar in the main square, which has had more names than I've had beers. Well, almost. The names reflect who had control of the town, from the Soviets who labelled it '4th April Square' in honour of when the Red Army liberated Bratislava from the Nazis to the Hungarians who called it Ferenc Jozsef Square at the start of the 20th century, and all the way back to the Romans who called it Forum Civitatis in the 17th century. I drink my beer and look up at the tower of the town hall, built in 1370 and wonder how many invaders it has witnessed.

We wander the old town for the afternoon, admiring the ornate buildings, the friendly compact nature of the place. On the Austrian side of town along the Danube, stylish glass-encased apartments are crowding the riverside. One juts out over the water as if the architect wants to somehow claim the mighty river as his own. We seek refuge from all this modernity in the narrow backstreets of the old town, among the many disused buildings waiting for new owners. It's ironic that while sleek futuristic eyesores are being erected a kilometre downstream, here in this beautiful town many buildings stand destitute and unloved. We climb the stairs to the castle and wander the grounds. Like the old town square, the castle has had many occupiers and undergone numerous incarnations. In fact, as recently as 1953 the place was a ruin and serious consideration was being given to demolishing it. Thankfully, the barbarians were convinced of its importance and a number of detailed restoration projects have been undertaken. It now operates as a museum and a major ceremonial site for Slovakian nationhood.

If there's one indisputable rule on how to find good food in popular tourist towns, it's to go where the tourists don't. That usually means stepping just outside the old town. Bratislava adheres to this rule not once, but twice.

Just a short hike up the hill from the old town towards the President's Palace is the lovely art deco Stefanka Cafe/Restaurant. We ate there last year and the owner allowed us to sit on the previously closed mezzanine level overlooking all the lunch time diners. We admired the cabinets full of crockery and memorabilia, lace covered tables, the wooden chairs on deep red carpet, the wonderfully old-fashioned heavy curtains and the grandfather clock in the corner. The owner took a shine to Cathie and kept offering her free wine. There's a lunch special every day which usually consists of soup, main course and dessert, often for less than E10 in total. The menu is typically Slovak with heavy dumpling and potato dishes, but the friendly atmosphere and beautiful decor make it worth a visit.

Except it's closed tonight, so we walk across the tram tracks to a microbrewery, Mestiansky Pivovar which offers pilsener-style beer and a mouth watering array of food to help wash down the lager. As usual, we order too much, beginning with a pork crackling paste accompanied by bread and onion. I count the slices of bread they offer with this dish. Eleven. For two people.

Cathie's main course is two duck legs with piles of red cabbage, dumplings and pancakes. Mine is chicken, liver and bacon in a stout beer sauce.

We eat half of each dish. Everything is delicious, but there is no way we can finish them. I think of asking for a doggy bag, but there aren't that many dogs in all of Bratislava.

The beer is pretty good as well.

We wander back into the old town, past the numerous restaurants offering such traditional Slovak food as pizza, chips and pork knuckle. And gelato.

Oh the humanity.

Accommodation: Avance Hotel, Bratislava. Modern hotel with large rooms, good wifi, standard breakfast, close to the old town and the river. My score: 15/20

Restaurant: Mestiansky Pivovar, Bratislava. A brewery which offers hearty meat and dumpling dishes washed down with good beer. Perhaps it's best to order just entrees which are large enough to be main courses. The bread is excellent. My score: 16/20

Distance cycled: 75 km

What I should have said: 'Can I exchange one duck leg for another beer, please?'

Chapter Twenty-one:

Bratislava to Velky Medev, Slovakia

We were tempted to stay another day in Bratislava, it's such an attractive and easy place to spend a sunny weekend. But I checked the weather for the next five days and a very wet, cold front is sweeping towards Budapest. By my calculation, the Hungarian capital is three days ride away. The front will hit in four days, so to dally here on a quiet Sunday could mean we'll suffer a damp entry into the capital of the Magyars.

So in record time we pack our panniers, eat a typically soulless bain marie hotel breakfast and hit the road. The plot for today is to keep north of the Danube and hope for more smooth surface levees to wile away the hours.

But first we must negotiate the maze of freeways. A Soviet-era stone sculpture surrounded by weeds and a few scraggly trees is opposite a new shopping centre with the impressive name of Europark selling the same plastic disposable rubbish as is sold everywhere in the first world. Next to Europark are two glass skyscrapers. Is this a perfect metaphor for the modern world? A glass building that remains steadfastly opaque while allowing us to see ourselves reflected back. Oh look at my new Prada handbag. Are these shoes the right colour? Do I really look like David Beckham with this new haircut?

It's a relief to locate the levee once again and join a few early morning skaters rolling along the smooth surface. Craig has been very quiet these past two days. I give his crossbar a little pat to show him I appreciate this brief respite from problems of a mechanical kind. He ignores me.

As we progress the river widens until it appears more like a lake with small islands and marshes and flocks of birds settling on the surface. Two geese fly past, their necks craned forward, like us beating into an increasingly stiff wind. I look across the lake. There are no hills anywhere on the horizon. We have entered a flat marsh plain, the wind whipping across the river with nothing to stop it except our fragile bodies. We hunker down and pedal that little bit harder. It reminds me very much of The Netherlands, atop a levee, a broad expanse of water to my right, a narrow canal to the left and not a hill in sight.

After two hours, we come down from the levee into Samorin, a town caught between high-rise apartments and modern suburban houses with a garden and vegetable patch. I'm not sure who's winning. We order two cakes - one chocolate, one hazelnut - from the local cafe. They are both superb and cost only a euro each. The owner makes a great coffee as well. I leave him a tip and he seems genuinely happy when I tell him how much I enjoyed his food. He says goodbye many times and wishes us a good day.

We wander back to the river via a modern hotel complex with a trendy bar, a lake, a children's playground and a small football field where a bunch of old blokes are playing five-a-side with as much vigour as you'd expect on a Sunday morning. Back on the levee, the wind continues unabated. A few kilometres along we decide to head to the nearest road down on the plain, away from the gusts. It's a smart decision. The wind continues all day and we get occasional relief from the roadside trees and buildings.

It's a major road, but is extremely well-designed featuring a 1.5 metre shoulder for bicycles and a solid white line with 'noise bumps' to alert motorists if they should stray into our turf. We pick up speed and decide to resist the charms of the Danube for the rest of the day.

The villages become less frequent as the small churches give way to endless advertising signs along the road. Kitchen appliances; an LCD television and a glass enclosure for your backyard swimming pool. We worship with the wallet and credit card now. The only advertising sign that brings a smile to my face is one that announces fellow Australian Kylie Minogue is appearing in Bratislava tonight, just as I'm leaving. I hope the star of daytime soap operas and raunchy music videos enjoys Bratislava as much as we did.

We stop in Dunajska Streda for lunch. The only place we can find that's open is a pizza joint. The friendly man dressed in black is extremely busy, but makes time for us. We order a calzone and a margherita, not expecting Italian magic in a lonely Slovak town. Truth is, they're better than some we've had in Italy. The calzone is twice the size we expected and full of ham, cheese, mushrooms and a crazy number of green olives. Cathie places them on the tray, like a child's collection of toy marbles. She pops one into her mouth every time I have a sip of beer. Spice for her, alcohol for me.

We have entered an area of Slovakia that is largely occupied by Hungarians. The region was ceded to Hungary in 1938 but after World War Two returned to the then Czechslovakia and on to Slovakia after the Velvet Divorce in 1993. There have been minor disputes since then, including an incident at a soccer match between the local team and Slovan Bratislava. I begin to notice signs in a number of languages.

The afternoon ride is wind and sun and old ladies foraging for hazelnuts on the ground, dropped from the roadside trees. We stop for water at a service station and when I enter a young woman is preening in front of a full length mirror, admiring her bottom in the tight jeans. She wears too much makeup and her fingernails are ferocious red. I think of her Grandmother by the side of the road scouring the earth for nuts, contemplating what meals she'll make with her pickings.

Then I decide I'm being too much of a negative old man. Why not allow the young an opportunity to shine in their brief moment of glamour and perfection. There's time enough for hazelnuts when we get old, when the flush of high cheekbones fade and the pert bottom sags. The three young men with the woman vie for her attention beside the fridge as I pay my money and take my leave, back to the rhythm of the road, the wind and the afternoon sun.

We arrive in Velky Meder, a spa town in Slovakia populated overwhelmingly by Hungarians - 84% at the last census. It's a curious town, little more than a village of pale stone houses and occasional shops until you reach the spa region on the outskirts. Here along the main road, nearly every house is large and newly built, each painted in a variety of gelato colours. All of them are pensions. Our pension for the night is called Pension Betty and is painted lime green. Next door is Pension Laguna, painted pale orange. Beside that is Pension Provence, a dubious mix of orange and yellow.

It looks unlike any spa town in which I've ever been. Most spa villages are nestled in narrow valleys or on mountain ridges and have ornate ancient baths. This is eye-poppingly modern, sleek and frankly, a little garish.

The owner is very friendly and proudly shows off the indoor swimming pool fed with spa water and the downstairs sauna. He offers us the choice of rooms, a small double bedroom or an apartment, both for the same price. He asks us when we'd like dinner and breakfast and I get the impression we're the only guests. Everything is modern and fresh and clean.

A sign informs us that our pension was part-funded with EU finances. I wonder how he's going to pay off the loan with such inexpensive room rates.

We change into our swimmers and enjoy the spa pool. The owner shows us how to operate the jacuzzi and the two huge shower heads that dump jet streams of water into the pool. All for just two guests.

The town of Velky Melder has a tragic history. In the First World War, thousands of Serb prisoners were held in a camp just outside of town. This area was part of the Austrian-Hungarian Empire and therefore at war with Serbia. Remember it was a Serb, Gavrilo Princip who was responsible for the assassination of the Austrian heir apparent, Archduke Franz Ferdinand in Sarejevo.

While the Serbs were being held prisoners here, a typhoid outbreak lead to the death of over five thousand men. They are buried in a mass grave just outside of town. No names or dates of death are recorded.

At dinner the owner greets us warmly and shows us into his restaurant decorated in shades of orange. We eat simple home-cooked meals, a sheep's cheese pasta and baked turkey breast, both served with salads of tomato, cucumber and lettuce.

When we return to our room in the evening, we notice the garish yellow, orange and pink strobe lighting in the lift shaft. Yes, this pension has a glass enclosed four storey lift. It's a disco hotel! Thankfully, our room is at the far end, well away from the light show. Again, I wonder how much all this infrastructure costs and if it's only for we two guests?

Perhaps it's busy in summer. I fall asleep wondering who is Betty? The owner's wife? Daughter? Does Betty mean something else in Slovak? Or Hungarian?

Accommodation: Pension Betty, Velky Melder. Friendly owner. Large rooms in a new building with wifi, garage for bicycles and an attached restaurant, spa pool and sauna. What's not to like, apart from the light show. My score: 16/20

Restaurant: Pension Betty, Velky Melder. Simple food based on pork, chicken and sheep cheese. Inexpensive. My score: 14/20

Distance cycled: 76 km

What I should have said: 'Is calzone a traditional Slovak dish, perhaps?'

Chapter Twenty-two:

Velky Meder to Sturovo, Slovakia

There are four workers in the breakfast room when we arrive this morning. I'm not sure why as we're the only guests. We are offered a choice of cooked breakfasts and wisely select the excellent scrambled eggs and ham. The chef, a large man with a goatee comes out and asks where we're heading and how far we've come. He is suitably impressed and we assure him his breakfast will give us the energy we need for today's ride.

It's cold and hazy this morning. A blue mist hangs over the fields, as if one hundred farmers are all having a cigarette in their tractors. The villages are more frequent than yesterday but strangely are not located on the main road. The church steeples remain a whisper on the horizon. Our constant companions are corn fields. It's been the same throughout the four countries since we started this journey. I have a sneaking suspicion that the corn is not for human consumption, but for the animals. I know I shouldn't object, but I prefer one stage in the food chain - that is, a cow eats grass and we eat the cow. The same for chickens - they eat insects in the grass and we eat the chickens. Industrial farming has demanded an extra step with the cows and chickens now fattened on grain, usually corn before going to the abattoir.

Call me an idealist, but I believe we should let animals eat what comes naturally to them. I'm happy to eat a cow that has lead a contented life in the paddocks munching on grass and feeling the sunshine on their backs. I do not want to eat an animal that has lived most of their life in a cage and been fattened for the sole purpose of my appetite. The presence of so many corn fields throughout Europe is not one I welcome.

The road is as good as yesterday, wide and impossibly flat. Thankfully today there's no roadside advertising. It's just us and the tractors. Entering the town of Komarno, I spy a child's playground which contains a rather confusing sculpture featuring a rocket ship, pitchforks and flowers. There's also an advert for the Komarno Fitness Grand Prix. It focuses on a woman in a bikini.

We walk down a narrow alley to a cafe which has a balcony with cushioned chairs and a small fountain. The sign on the door says it opens at 10:30 am. The waitress ushers us in, even though it's not even 10 am. The owner is a friendly chap who speaks a little English and he encourages us to try a traditional Hungarian cake. We order two. The cake is reminiscent of a trifle with a mix of chocolate and vanilla sponge cake, fruit and nuts and cream. I take three bites and walk back into the cafe from our balcony table to tell the owner how delicious it is. We're still in Slovakia of course, but if this is any indication of what to expect from Hungarian cafes, I can't wait. I also order a half-litre jug of home-made lemonade. I've spent too long eating in restaurants and my stomach is starting to feel the effects. Doesn't stop me ordering cake though.

After Komarno, we return to a wide smooth path on the levee beside the river. It allows us to crank up the speed, from slow to medium-slow and watch the sluggish Danube meander along. We detour into the village of Radvan nad Dunajom, which has an intriguing monument of six bells hanging from a three-legged iron structure. It's the Peace of Zsitvatorok Memorial commemorating the signing of an agreement ending the thirty years war between the Ottoman Empire and the Hapburgs on November 11th 1606. It was erected in 2006 to celebrate the 400th anniversary.

I love history, but it strikes me as somewhat unusual that a Memorial celebrating a peace deal four centuries ago between two foreign powers is given such prominence in a Slovak town. Until I learn that 91% of residents in this town categorise themselves as Hungarian. There's no more fervent nationalist than a displaced nationalist. I wonder if the bells of the Memorial are rung every week? Or month? Or only on the anniversary? Or perhaps they are cunningly designed to ring every time a fair wind blows across the Danube from the Hungarian Motherland? There is no mention of Slovakia on the Memorial or on any of the attached information boards.

As we set off again on the levee, I look across the Danube. This village was once a fishing port on the river. I imagine a resident of the town today rowing his boat out to mid-stream where the Slovak-Hungarian border line nominally exists. Does the fisherman cast his line into the Hungarian depths and catch only fish from his spiritual homeland? Or does he cunningly amuse himself by stealing fish from the Slovaks?

For lunch, we stop at the intriguingly named Fish Boat Paradise Restaurant aboard a moored houseboat parked at a marina. Once again, we are the only guests. Cathie orders whole grilled trout and I order catfish, assuming it's caught straight from the Danube flowing under the pontoons. I ask the waitress if this is true. She shrugs her shoulders. It comes from a freezer in the kitchen.

It's a lovely location, looking across to the small Hungarian village of Labatlan. There's an identical looking pontoon on the opposite bank, but it's too far away for me to tell whether it houses a similar restaurant. Our restaurant plays nameless 90s pop music which is the bane of our dining experience in Europe. No, I don't really expect endless Hungarian folk tunes or Slovakian battle hymns, but I'd like to occasionally hear a foreign singing voice on European airwaves, rather than endless English or American pap.

The fish is much better than the music.

Back on the levee Craig starts complaining again, this time

refusing to change gears properly. I fiddle with his adjustments and he gets worse. I fiddle some more and twenty kilometres from our hotel, he relents and starts behaving. In fact, as we turn off the levee onto a back road, he senses the wind is at our backs and positively speeds away. It's as if he's a racehorse and has finally sniffed home. Cathie and Jenny gamely keep up and we complete the last few kilometres in no time at all.

From a distance, the Esztergom Basicila can be seen towering over the landscape, its massive green dome like a beacon on the headland above the river.

We quickly check into our pension down a small street in Sturovo, not far from the bridge separating the two countries. We don't even bother to shower, deciding to enter the realms of Hungary's largest Catholic Church in our lycra and hoping we won't be struck down for the sacrilege. It's a lovely cycle over the green bridge into Hungary and up the hill to the Basilica. The sun is setting behind the dome as we bounce on the cobblestones. I'm struck by how few people are here. From the front, the Basilica looks like a heavily pillared fortress with oversized green double doors that appear as if they haven't been opened in years. We make our entrance through a side door.

The Basilica is correctly titled the Primatial Basilica of the Blessed Virgin Mary Assumed Into Heaven and St Adalbert. It has a simple yet elegant interior of red and white marble with numerous Tuscan Renaissance motifs.

It also houses the crypt of the former Hungarian Archbishop and hero Jozef Mindszenty who dedicated his life to the church and opposing Nazi and Communist rulers in his homeland. For his views he was imprisoned and tortured before being briefly released during the uprising of 1956. When the Soviets invaded soon after, Mindszenty sought and was given refuge in the American embassy in Budapest where he stayed for fifteen years before being exiled to

Austria shortly before his death in 1975. His remains were repatriated to Esztergom soon after the fall of communism. He remains a well-respected figure in modern Hungary.

We wander the quiet interior, admiring the work of Italian artist Michelangelo Grigoletti who painted the altar showpiece, the Assumption of Mary, reputedly the largest altarpiece in the world painted on a single canvas.

The Basilica is massive church, only surpassed in Europe by St Peter's in Rome and Saint Paul's Cathedral in London. And yet, its very simplicity gives it a much more human scale. Or is it the lack of people sharing the hallowed interior with us? We look up at the dome and gaze open mouthed in wonder. Such majesty and beauty.

The sun is shimmering on the Danube as we walk around the grounds, high on a bluff near the river. A single cruise boat is moored below us, unloading a line of camera-toting tourists, all gazing upwards to the Basilica.

It's time for more delicious Hungarian cakes down in the lower town of Esztergom, in a pretty square crowded with students walking home from college. A young man in a peaked cap rides slowly beside his girlfriend in jeans and a t-shirt. He wobbles in the seat because they're holding hands and he has to stretch to maintain her clasp. They giggle.

The green domed Basilica towers above the town. I eat an excellent apple cake and wonder why I feel guilty. Too many cafes, not enough churches?

We cycle back to our pension in the much less interesting town of Sturovo on the Slovakian side of the river. Alcohol shops, all night gambling and a pedestrian thoroughfare without many people make the place seem desolate and forgotten. On one side of the river is a world famous Basilica and wealthy tourists alighting from a cruise ship. On this side, two young men drink beer outside a pub and eat hamburgers and chips.

The streets seem darker, the smell of sewerage hangs in the air and I wonder how many people are behind the opaque walls of the all night gambling den?

We return to our pension and think about tomorrow, our last day on the Danube.

Accommodation: Pension Everlast, Sturovo. The owner wears an Everlast t-shirt, offers me an Everlast energy drink on arrival and has an Everlast punching bag hanging in the courtyard. Apart from that, the wifi works well, it's a large somewhat old apartment and there's no breakfast offered. It's a budget choice. My score: 13/20

Dinner: El Camino Restaurant, Sturovo. Excellent fish soup, good deep-fried camembert and passable risotto served in a large open room with, you guessed it, 90s music playing in the background. My score: 14/20

Distance cycled: 85 km

What I should have said: 'How much does the Everlast sponsorship bring in?'

Chapter Twenty-three:

Sturovo, Slovakia to Budapest, Hungary

We wake to pouring rain and the sad news from home that our political hero, Gough Whitlam, Prime Minister of Australia from 1972-75 has died at the age of ninety-eight. Mr Whitlam and his Labor Party initiated reforms that allowed a working class boy such as myself the opportunity to attend university and be paid for the privilege. His government introduced Aboriginal Lands Rights legislation; was the first to diplomatically recognise China; instituted a universal health care scheme and immediately brought home the troops from Vietnam. He was a tremendous orator and had a fiercely independent intellect. Perhaps he was the greatest Australian. I shed a tear this morning before heading out into the inclement weather.

The mist clouds the hills on both sides of the Danube as we plot a route along a path strewn with wet leaves and the occasional fallen branch. A few hardy fishermen have driven their cars onto the sand beside the river to try their luck. They bunker down in full length raincoats on chairs and look out into the river. I wonder if catfish is their prize?

The path yields to a road running beside the river. It's potholed and populated by too many aggressive Audi drivers so we stick close to the edge and listen keenly for approaching cars. At Visegrad, there's a garish theme park in front of the lower castle. Plastic and brightly painted wood obscuring the artistry and history of over five centuries.

We stop at a restaurant to escape the downpour, parking our bikes among the outdoor furniture under an awning. The owner ushers us inside. He explains that he's not open until midday. It's

10 am. We apologise but he shakes his head and offers us coffee. We push our luck and order apple cheesecake and pancakes as well. The cakes are delicious, the coffee hot and when we look outside we see blue sky for the first time. We're sure it's an omen due to the kindness of this restaurant owner.

By the time we shrug back into our jackets the sun is shining and we're feeling much happier. My son has posted on his twitter feeds one of the great quotes of Mr Whitlam. When someone jeered him at a public meeting and yelled, 'What are you going to do about abortion?' Mr Whitlam swiftly responded, 'In your case, I'd make it retrospective.' Although perhaps my favourite Whitlam quote, written for a newspaper many years ago was, 'I've never said I'm immortal. I do believe in correct language. I'm eternal; I'm not immortal.' Never was a truer word written. Gough shall be remembered in Australian history forever.

Back on the road and Hungarian drivers seem to be somewhat more cavalier than their Slovakian counterparts. Too often, cars pass Cathie and I with only a few inches to spare. At our next stop, it gives Cathie a chance to vent her latest theory.

'The worse the infrastructure, the more dangerous the driver,' she says.

'Maybe it's just the infrastructure that makes them appear so inconsiderate,' I answer.

She shakes her head. 'No, it's about competing for limited space. They become more aggressive because they have such little space. They want to claim it all as their own.'

We both sigh and head back onto the road. Finally, a Euro Velo 6 sign appears leading us away from the battleground and down towards the river. The path is slippery with leaves and takes us past an odd assortment of Hungarian industries, including an old Army barracks with rusting drill equipment, missiles stacked three high and a fleet of very old trucks that await the scrap merchant.

'Those missiles are empty, I imagine,' I say.

'How do you empty a missile?' Cathie asks.

'Hold it upside down and shake,' I suggest.

The path continues to get worse, so bad now that I take the dirt track worn into the grass beside the bitumen rather than deal with all the potholes. It's a rather inauspicious entrance into Budapest, which by my calculation is only ten kilometres away.

Suddenly the path improves and we cycle past numerous closed restaurants and a kayak centre before stopping outside a very sleek and modern 'wellness centre.' A restaurant is attached to the multi-storey complex. Through the double-glazed windows, we can see businessmen dining. We park Craig and Jenny near the front entrance in the sun and enter nervously.

The host welcomes us as if we're long standing customers and leads us to a table near the window. We trail footprints of dirt and mud wherever we go.

He hands us the menu and in excellent English tells us he'll be back soon to take our order. All thoughts of aggressive Hungarian motorists disappear in the time it takes to order a hamburger for me and a pumpkin soup for Cathie. The waiter brings us an amuse bouche to begin our meal. I love that. Anything free always wins me over. The food is delicious, the view sensational and the businessmen ignore us as we tuck into the food. The waiter teaches us how to say 'thank you' 'good' and 'delicious' in Hungarian. We are primed for our entry into Budapest.

Which despite his friendliness, remains somewhat fraught. We somehow end up on an island in the Danube, cycling along wide empty roads until we reach a dead-end. We return to the mainland over a ricketty Soviet-era bridge and consider our next move. We shakily lug our bikes across a train track and cycle on the footpath of a very busy road. I can see the Danube off to my left. So near. On a backstreet, we pass a coffee shop called 'My little

Melbourne.' I'm tempted to go in and see if an Australian runs the place and can give us cycle-friendly directions to the centre of his or her adopted capital city.

Finally by chance we come upon a sign leading us back to the cycle path on the Danube. We both breathe a sigh of relief. It means a lot to us to enter this final city of our trip in the correct way. We stop opposite the imposing and grand Parliament Building and have our photo taken with Jenny and Craig. We are muddy and dishevelled, but proud we've finally made it here, all the way from Basel in Switzerland. Not even last year's tragic flood could deter us from finishing this journey. I kiss Cathie and give both Jenny and Craig a celebratory pat.

We cross the Elizabeth Bridge and despite the hectic traffic find our apartment located in a wonderful neighbourhood. Opposite our apartment is the second most popular restaurant in Budapest - a soup kitchen that is legendary. Downstairs is a ramen restaurant and two buildings away is the most famous pub in town. Young beautiful hipsters walk by as we wait for the owner of the apartment to arrive. She is suitably glamourous and friendly. The apartment is on the first floor and looks over the street. It's fully equipped with everything we need, including a washing machine. We are both tremendously excited about washing our clothes in a proper machine rather than in a hotel sink.

All this is ours for three days at the ridiculously cheap price of one hundred and thirty-five euros. We can't believe our luck.

At night, we eat in the ramen restaurant and the food is impossibly cheap and tasty. The place is populated by good looking young people dressed in black. And two Australians who could be their grandparents, also dressed in black. It's the most appropriate colour for pannier touring.

Over the next three days, we wander the streets of Budapest, checking out all the tourist sights. It's a pleasure to not have to pack our clothes into the panniers every morning, to not have to plot a route in and out by bicycle, to be able to retire to an apartment in the middle of the day and fall asleep on the lounge, dribbling and dreaming of cycling beside the Danube with Craig not causing any mechanical problems.

Winter has arrived early in Budapest. The wind howls down the wide boulevards, the locals dress in full-length jackets and fur-lined headgear. It's the perfect weather for soup. So we join the line outside the restaurant/soup kitchen opposite. I'm the oldest person in the line by thirty years. I can't understand the soup menu, so order the top two from a board advertising six choices. I also order a toasted baguette, which sounds rather pedestrian. Who toasts baguettes?

We take the food back to our apartment and eat it while watching the line downstairs grow longer. Cathie's soup is broccoli, mine chicken with coriander. It's a little hard to describe soup. Hot, tasty, nourishing - it's just soup. Only this soup is like the nectar of the gods. It is sensational, displaying a depth of flavour and quality of ingredients that makes me want to rush out and order some more. Except I have a toasted baguette to eat. It's crunchy with spicy fresh chicken and a distinctive light sauce that tastes almost like ... like soup on a roll! Cathie and I shake our heads in wonder. All this for the equivalent of six euro.

After eating, I write to the owner of our apartment and ask for an extension for three more days. Yes we want to see the sights of Budapest but really it's the soup that forces us to linger. We learn soon after that the chef is a Michelin-starred artist who decided to set up his own place and cater for we ordinary folk rather than the rich and famous. I love his food and his food politics.

If I have to nominate my two favourite Budapest haunts, apart from a certain soup kitchen, it's Momento Park on the outskirts of the city and the Thermal Baths.

Momento Park was established a few years after the parting of the Iron Curtain. Budapest was littered with many Soviet-era statues that reminded the newly-freed citizens of a recent past they wanted to forget. Some of the statues were destroyed, but luckily many were preserved and are now housed in what can only be described as a Communist Theme Park.

What is it about Soviet-era art? The triumph of the worker. The beauty of the machine. Is it the combination of exultation and threat, the great leap forward or bodies crushed under tanks? I'm sure if I'd lived in communist Hungary in the 60s and 70s, I wouldn't find these monuments so appealing. Nowhere have I seen a statue with such daunting power and brute force as the nine-metre tall Republic of Councils Monument depicting a single worker brandishing a flag and a fist as he strides forward to smite the revisionists and traitors. Wherever I walk in the park, his eyes and fists follow me, a Mona Lisa of the masses.

Across the patchy gardens is the Bela Kun Memorial, in Socialist Realism bronze and shimmering steel, where the People's Commissar for Foreign Affairs in the ill-fated first Hungarian Soviet Republic of 1919 stands beside an old-fashioned lamp-post above a crowd of soldiers exhorting them to attack, bayonets drawn, chins jutting forward, forever ready. Brutal and beautiful, triumphant but cliched, it's achingly timeless yet rooted in a failed Soviet age.

All these warriors of a generation stand in dissolute formation, glowering at the tourists who take photographs and wonder what the heck that era was all about?

After all this majesty and malevolence we welcome the chance to sit behind the wheel of a Trabant, two cylinders of spluttering ideology, affectionate symbol of the fall of the wall. Old communist joke. 'How do you double the value of a Trabant?' Fill up the tank.

Momento Park is wonderful trip back to a recent past, when statues were given such names as 'The Republic of Councils Pioneers Memorial plaque' and 'The Display of the Worker's Militia Monument.' No doubt, Lenin is rolling in his grave to see how his bold plans for a people's society lead first to dictatorship and suppression and now to outright exploitation in the form of a tourist park. Don't worry Vladimir, capitalism may have 'won' but perhaps one day the workers will rise up again and install a real people's party, free from the shackles of Communist dogma or Corporatist exploitation.

And so to the ultimate rich person's indulgence - a soak in a hot pool at the Thermal Baths. Budapest has quite a few of these regal old buildings. We choose the Szechenyi Medicinal Baths in City Park. Opened in 1913, it's the largest thermal baths in Europe. Baroque in style, it houses three outdoor and twelve indoor pools, fed by two mineral springs.

I'm not a fan of thermal baths. Hundreds of overweight and unhealthy people sitting around collectively in hot water is not my idea of a good time. All I see is the potential of catching tinea; ear, nose and throat infections or an upper respiratory illness.

But my beautiful wife has cycled thousands of kilometres alongside me through wind and rain and cold and if she wants to soak in a hot pool, than it would be churlish not to join her. We bypass the indoor pools where hundreds of semi-naked people soak in hot pools with barely any room to move. Instead we venture out into the rain and the five degree outdoors to the larger pools. Steam rises from the surface. I nervously enter the hot water and slowly but surely start to relax. It's fun having cold raindrops fall on my head while the rest of my body is soaking in a comfortable thirty-eight degrees celsius.

'I knew you'd enjoy it,' Cathie says.

'It'd be fun in the snow,' I answer.

We hop out and immediately start shivering. We walk briskly to the outdoor circular pool at the far end of the complex. This pool shoots jets of water in an anti-clockwise motion. We join the few people being pushed around the pool by the jacuzzi tide. It's hilarious, like being a child again on a water slide. We're pushed in a large circle whether we like it or not. We like it. I can't help but smile. Cathie smiles back. Once again, my beautiful wife is proven right.

The second last day of our stay is October 23rd, a public holiday in Hungary to celebrate the 1956 revolution when it seemed for a brief few weeks that Hungary would leave the Soviet Bloc and become an independent country under Prime Minister Irme Nagy. Alas, the Soviets invaded and brutally repressed the uprising, leading to the deaths of hundreds of protestors and freedom fighters and the subsequent execution of Irme Nagy with his body being buried unceremoniously in an unmarked grave. It was not until 1989 and the 31st anniversary of Nagy's execution that he was reburied with full honours.

To celebrate October 23rd, the Parliament Building and the so-called 'House of Terror' - a museum detailing the Soviet crimes in Hungary - are both free to the public. The queue for each stretches for a kilometre, proving that the citizens haven't forgotten the events of the first half of the 20th century. Apart from these two displays, the streets are relatively quiet with a gathering of people at the bronze statue of Imre Nagy. His statue stands on a small bridge over a fountain, his head is turned to the left looking towards Parliament and perhaps a future where the people could choose who resided in that building.

We walk to the train station and try to purchase tickets back to

France, where we'll fly home. The young blonde woman behind the counter shakes her head when we mention we have two bicycles.

'Very difficult,' she says.

'They're just bicycles,' I reply.

She stabs away at the computer for what seems like hours, checking timetables, routes, constantly shaking her head. She explains that the season is over and direct trains don't accommodate bicycles in autumn and winter. The thought occurs to me that if we packed Jenny and Craig in two boxes perhaps we could sneak them aboard as luggage.

Finally she plots a route which allows Jenny and Craig to return east with us. It requires a rather depressing early morning start and the changing of trains on seven occasions. I can't quite believe that in modern Europe, we are being forced onto regional and suburban trains because of two bicycles. There is nothing to be done but shrug and buy the tickets. Which takes an hour as the poor woman has to hand-write a bicycle ticket for every stage of the journey through four countries. She is extremely careful about each stage and makes sure we have all the appropriate details. We'll begin in Budapest at 5:20am and hopefully arrive in Strasbourg at midnight. I sigh. It's an inglorious way to finish our journey.

No matter, it's a celebration day for Hungary so we take to the streets and wander this beautiful city of so many lovely buildings and the ever-flowing Danube with young lovers walking along its banks. I photograph the long queue of free people waiting to enter the biggest Parliament building in the world. The queue moves slowly yet deliberately forward.

We enter another coffee shop called 'My little Melbourne' which serves excellent coffee. I'm mystified by an apparent chain of Australian coffee shops in Budapest. The workers are Hungarian but the walls are littered with speedos, an Australian football jersey, a kangaroo road-crossing sign and other kitsch paraphernalia.

It makes me feel homesick.

Perhaps it's time to return home.

Accommodation: Colours Apartments, Kazinczy 9, Budapest. Wonderful spacious apartments at budget prices with excellent wifi, cooking facilities, garage for bicycles and a very helpful host. Can be noisy at night, but the apartment has soundproof windows, air-conditioning and shutters. My score: 18/20

Dinner: I'd recommend three restaurants within fifty metres of the apartment. Bors Gsztrobar offers sublime soups and baguettes for ridiculously cheap prices. Ramenka Restaurant serves excellent ramen and Japanese dishes. And for coffee, Szimplakerti Haztaji, a long name for a simple cafe serving excellent food and good coffee.

Distance cycled: 75 km

What I should have said: 'Don't think of them as bicycles. They're just movable hand-luggage.'

Printed in Great Britain
by Amazon.co.uk, Ltd.,
Marston Gate.